MW00960785

GRAYSVILLE

YOU CAN'T GET THERE
WHEN THE CREEK RISES

Other books:
Gray's Island, Where the Creek Bends

GRAYSVILLE

YOU CAN'T GET THERE
WHEN THE CREEK RISES

SHIRLEY BROCK TURNEY

authorHOUSE®

AuthorHouse™
1663 Liberty Drive
Bloomington, IN 47403
www.authorhouse.com
Phone: 1 (800) 839-8640

© 2015 Shirley Brock Turney. All rights reserved.

Front and Back Cover photos by: Shirley Turney
Photos by: Richard Turney and Shirley Turney

No part of this book may be reproduced, stored in a retrieval system, or
transmitted by any means without the written permission of the author.

Published by AuthorHouse 09/17/2015

ISBN: 978-1-5049-2678-2 (sc)
ISBN: 978-1-5049-2677-5 (e)

Library of Congress Control Number: 2015912401

Print information available on the last page.

Any people depicted in stock imagery provided by Thinkstock are models,
and such images are being used for illustrative purposes only.
Certain stock imagery © Thinkstock.

This book is printed on acid-free paper.

Because of the dynamic nature of the Internet, any web addresses or links contained in
this book may have changed since publication and may no longer be valid. The views
expressed in this work are solely those of the author and do not necessarily reflect the
views of the publisher, and the publisher hereby disclaims any responsibility for them.

KJV
Scripture quotations marked KJV are from the Holy Bible, King James Version
(Authorized Version). First published in 1611. Quoted from the KJV Classic
Reference Bible, Copyright © 1983 by The Zondervan Corporation.

DEDICATION

I dedicate this book in loving memory of my sister, Peggy Ann Brock Branam, who passed away before it was finished.

For my grandchildren, John Patrick, Elizabeth, Jason, William and Mary Grace

CONTENTS

ACKNOWLEDGEMENTS

I thank my family and friends for their support during the writing of this book. After publishing Gray's Island where the Creek Bends, I was encouraged to write another book with more Graysville history and childhood stories. Again, I must thank my brothers and sisters who helped me make these memories. A special thank you goes to my dear friend, Ms Rebecca Eaves, who has inspired me to continue writing and for all her help with the history of Graysville. I want to thank my good friend and editor, Beverely Houchins, for all her commas and semi-colons. I also want to thank my brother Bill who has sold more of my books than I have.

Above all, I want to thank my husband John for his support and encouragement in my efforts to write this book. Also, thank you to my sons and their wives, Richard and Martha, Peter and Alice.

Thanks guys. Again, I hope that I make you proud.

ABOUT THE AUTHOR

I was born in Hawkinsville, Georgia. Around the age of four, our family moved to Graysville, Georgia, where I grew up. After I graduated from Ringgold High School, I held several jobs. In later years, I attended Chattanooga State Community College. I also worked for friends in their bookkeeping and tax service business.

Through the years, I have done lots of volunteer work at school and church. I spend much of my time helping others in need. I am a devoted wife, mother, grandmother and animal lover. Besides my grandchildren, my passion is making quilts. This is my second book. I have no formal training or writing experience, but I do not let that stop me. I never meet a stranger, and like Will Rogers, I have never met anyone I did not like. My favorite saying is, "Spend your money and enjoy life. There will be no Wells Fargo truck following the hearse to the cemetery."

INTRODUCTION

This book is a collection of childhood memories, poems and life in a simpler time during the early days of Graysville. It is about when Graysville was nothing more than an Indian village, the time Mr. Gray brought industry to the area, the civil war, the hardship of life back in the early 1900's and up to the present day. Graysville was, and still is, no ordinary small community. Each family has their own unique personalities that make them different from each other. With the blessings of several local families, they have shared their own stories with me for the book. Most of the stories have been passed down from generation to generation, so I do not know how accurate they are. Some of the stories are from my own experiences growing up in Graysville, and I am not sure if I remember them correctly. However accurate they are, I want to preserve them in my book since they most likely will not be found in the local library archives.

HISTORY AND
BACKGROUND

GRAYSVILLE HISTORY

In the beginning, God created the heavens and the earth, and He created Graysville, Georgia. It was not the Garden of Eden; but according to some, it was close. I guess it all comes down to the fact that being born in Graysville is what makes it so special. People passing through may wonder why we think it is such a terrific place. As I always say, "You just had to grow up in Graysville to understand."

Graysville is a small community in the north corner of Catoosa County near the Tennessee state line. It is a narrow valley that lies between two ridges beside the Chickamauga creek and the railroad. It was an Indian village until 1838 when the Indian Removal Act forced them to leave. Mr. Gray brought the railroad through and decided to settle there himself. It became a township in 1849 and began to boom when Mr. Gray brought in his businesses. Graysville always had a post office, general store and a school. Near the springs, there was also a stockade where civil war prisoners were held. The foundation can still be seen. The Church family was the first white settlers in Graysville. They were there when Mr. Gray came. They had several slaves, and some of them are buried in the Graysville Cemetery. The two brothers, Frank and Mark Church, were stonemasons. They built the gristmill and other buildings for Mr. Gray. The Church brothers were the best stonemasons, and no one could cut or set a stone like them. They certainly did a good job on the old gristmill. They could have never imagined what a beautiful home it would become.

Mr. Gray donated the land for the Graysville Methodist Church and the Graysville Cemetery. There are some old unmarked graves in the cemetery. Back then people who could not afford to buy a tombstone just marked the grave with a rock. As years passed, rocks were moved and people forgot where the graves were.

The Blackwell family was another family that moved to Graysville sometime around 1834. They settled in with the Indians in the area around Graysville Methodist Church. At that time, the Methodist Church was named Blackwell Chapel. The Cherokee Indians lived all around Graysville, especially the springs and along the creek bank. Graysville was originally named "Opelika" by the Indians. Graysville was also called "Pull Tight" by the early settlers because the roads were so muddy when it rained it was hard to travel. Two of the Indians living near the springs were "Wulukin" and Scrapeshin." The ridge running through Graysville was knows as Scrapeshin Ridge. There is also a street named after Chief Scrapeshin in the Council Fire subdivision.

Cherokee leader, Drowning Bear, lived along the South Chickamauga Creek in the area of the Audubon Acres. Among the other people living in the Graysville and East Brainerd areas, was an Indian named "Fields." He had a home and trading post on a farm that was later known as the Ira Dobbin place. Mrs. Fields was the sister of Chief John Ross. A man named McCoy, whose wife was also a sister of Chief Ross, lived near a mound on the Blackwell Farm. The Ross girls had been educated at the Brainerd Mission. A white man named "North" lived near the cemetery on the Blackwell Farm. His wife was a full blooded Indian named "Culstiah." There was also a man named "Braname" who settled the place later know as the Mackie Farm. This is where a beautiful old house was turned into the Narrowbridge Restaurant, which is no longer in business. The Indian Too Ni lived near the Walnut Grove spring on South Gunbarrel Road about one half mile from East Brainerd Road. A Cherokee Council Ground was located near the spring on the Blackwell-Ellis Farm. Today it is known as the Rhodes Farm. It is bordered by Davidson and Julian Road. Spring Frog and Little Owl were among the Indians living at Audubon Acres. Draggin Canoe, brother of Little Owl, also lived in the area for a while. He was a great warrior and did not stay any one place very long. Chief Kulstatee lived on the Blackwell farm property.

Back in the 1800s, some of the other families that lived in Graysville besides the Blackwells, were the Church family; and, of course, Mr. Gray and family and John F. Reynolds. He was an agent of the Western and

Atlantic Railroad and worked for Mr. Gray. Wesley Rhodes, and Dr. Blackford, who built the Graysville house, also lived there. Most of these people are buried in the Graysville Cemetery.

This information was compiled in 1993 by Rebecca R. Eaves from recollections, written and oral, of Cynthia Warlick Ellis, whose grandfather William Blackwell moved here from Hall County, Georgia, in 1834. His farm on the Tennessee Georgia line was located on South Chickamauga Creek about two miles from Graysville. Today this land is the Council Fire Golf Course.

CHEROKEE INDIANS

Graysville was a Cherokee Indian village back in the early 1800s. The little settlement was known as Opelika. The Opelika post office name was changed to Graysville post office in 1856. The name Opelika comes from the Creek Indians. When translated into English it means "Great Swamp or Big Swamp" because there was an abundant supply of water. The early settlers also called the area "Pull Tight." A group of Cherokee Indians lived along the creek banks until 1838 when they were forced to join the Trail of Tears. The Cherokee Indians roamed the Chickamauga Creek banks in Graysville long before the early settlers came. It was a perfect place for the Indians to live. The area was a bounty of wild game, fish and fresh water springs surrounded by the creek, hills, fields and trees. I can imagine the Indians in their native clothing, fishing and walking up and down the creek bank looking for fresh deer tracks and other wild game. That is probably why so many arrowheads washed up on Gray's Island. Deer, turkeys, coyotes and other wild animals still roam around Graysville in the early morning hours. Mrs. Poston even saw a fox one morning. When I visit Graysville and the springs, it feels like I am walking around in the footprints of the Indians. When my brother restored the springs back to their natural landscape, he preserved the very grounds the Indians called home for hundreds maybe thousands of years. If only those springs could talk, what a story they could tell. After a visit to the springs, it inspires me to take away a peaceful feeling of how it must have been in their time.

When Andrew Jackson was elected president in 1828, it was the beginning of the end for the Indians. President Andrew Jackson signed the Indian Removal Act in 1830. This Act gave the Federal Government the power to exchange Native-held land east of the Mississippi for land to the West, which later became the state of Oklahoma. The Cherokee did fight for their land by filing lawsuits that went as high as the Supreme Court. At this time, the Indians were no longer savages. They had log cabin homes, farms, stores and other shops. However, President Jackson continued to force the

Indians off their land. In 1817, many of the Indians gave up their land and moved to Arkansas and by 1828, they had moved on to Oklahoma. The Federal Government began enforcing the Removal Act and by 1838 the last of the Indians were moved to their new Indian territory west of the Mississippi River. This was their promised land. Tragically, in later years they were again forced to leave a place they called home.

Cherokee leader, Drowning Bear, lived in the Spring Frog Cabin and was forced to leave on the Trail of Tears. The Indians were terribly upset about leaving their homes and land. The Cherokee joined with the Seminole, Chickasaw, Creek, Choctaw and other Indian tribes on the Trail of Tears. Mothers, fathers and children were heartbroken and felt so badly they all cried. They said nothing, just hung their heads and sadly kept on going west leaving behind a trail of tears. The reason it is called the Trail of Tears is that the Indians cried all the way to Oklahoma leaving a trail of tears. The removal of the Indians from their native land, along with the civil war, were the darkest chapters in American history. In both, much suffering was endured all because of greed that over ruled compassion for human rights.

Along the trail, the Indians faced harsh weather, difficult times and even death, but had to trudge on toward the promise of a new land. Due to the cold winters and hot summers, diseases and starvation many of them died along the way. This was a sad and dark time for the Cherokee and other tribes caused by the actions of President Jackson and other white settlers who drove them away from their ancestral homeland. It was all because the white settlers wanted the Indian's land to farm. In 1828, the first American gold rush in the North Georgia Mountains also contributed to taking the land from the Cherokee.

Oklahoma was to be their new home and Promised Land given to them by the Federal Government to last for forever, but it never happened. As the white settlers encroached on the Indian's land beyond the Mississippi River, Oklahoma soon became a state. Again, the Indians were forced to relocate farther west.

Today we have a better understanding of their culture and struggles. The Indian days in Graysville were a unique time in history when cultures were different along with beliefs and values that no longer exist. It was a time that will never be seen again unless some great catastrophe happens that destroys most of humanity. The ones left will have to go back to living off the land like in the early days of Graysville. Comparing the standards of the 1800s to life today would certainly be like stepping back into another world in which most of us could not survive. It is a powerful and important story for all of us to remember. History does have a tendency of repeating itself. This land is your land, this land is my land, but this land rightfully belongs to the Native American Indians who were settled here long before the white man appeared. With all the immigrants migrating into the United States one day we might be singing this land is your land, this land is no longer my land. How sad that would be if some day America should fall. God bless America.

MR. GRAY COMES
TO GRAYSVILLE

Graysville has so much history to be such a small place. John David Gray did not know what kind of future and memories this place would hold when he settled there in the mid 1800s. Mr. Gray's arrival in Graysville was the beginning of a new age for the primitive area. Mr. Gray was a major contractor for the Western and Atlantic Railroad Company. He was awarded a contract to build the first railroad from Dalton, Georgia, to Chattanooga, Tennessee, which was completed in May 1850. Mr. Gray and his brothers, William and Robert were builders of railroads. The brothers had a huge enterprise that involved many other businesses all over the Southern states. Their company received the major contract for the construction of the South Caroline Railroad, which was the first railroad in the South. William stayed in Macon working on railroads while John D. and Robert came to North Georgia. The railroad was intended to replace the Old Federal Road that ran through Georgia. The Old Federal Road was a trading route used by the Indians and the white settlers. It was the first road through Catoosa County and Indian Territory. It ran from, Augusta, Georgia, and along the way near Chattanooga, it split and went to Nashville and Knoxville. It was heavily used both by Indians and by white settlers to move cargo through the state. In the early days when Mr. Gray brought the railroad through Graysville, he was so fond of the area that he bought a large amount of land on the South Chickamauga Creek. He laid out a town with streets that still exist today. That is how Graysville was founded in 1849. John D. Gray and family lived on the hill somewhere in the area of where the Swansons now live. He made a home for his family and started developing the area with several of his businesses. Some of the businesses were the Mining and Manufacturing Company which was a huge brick building that extended from Front Street almost all the way back to Gray Street. Just behind the manufacturing building was a small block building that was used for the voting precinct and the mayor's office. This building housed a furniture factory and many other businesses through the years. Mr. Gray also built a big, three-story gristmill that was used to grind grain. He also built a distillery that was destroyed by a storm, which was probably an answer to the prayers of many of the Graysville women.

His limestone business was near the Chickamauga Creek across from Graysville. Part of the oven where the limestone was made is still standing. The limestone was kept going in a hot furnace day and night. The limestone was carried by a pulley across the creek. It was then shipped by the Graysville Mining and Manufacturing Company. He also developed a barrel company to ship the limestone. Apparently, Mr. Gray did not believe in the middleman. If he needed something, he just formed a company and made whatever he needed.

There were many people living in the Graysville area, and no doubt most of them worked for Mr. Gray. He paid his employees with scrip paper or coins. These were used instead of money and could only be used in the company store. Since Graysville was so far out in the wilderness, it was hard to keep cash money on hand. It was easier to issue scrip payments since the people had nowhere else to shop and spend their money. A few years ago, Dickie Fryar found several of these scrip coins in a load of dirt he was using to fill in some holes in his yard. They are one of his prized possessions.

The Opelika post office name was changed to Graysville post office in 1856. Robert Gray was postmaster at the time. The post office was in a small room at the front of the Mining and Manufacturing building. Across the street, there was a depot where the train stopped to let people off and pick up new passengers going either north or south. Most of the passengers were drummers who traveled to Chattanooga or Ringgold on business. There was a large water tank where the steam engines filled up with water to make steam to push the trains on down the track. One cold winter in the 1940s, the water in the pipes froze. The train could not get water for the steam engine. Someone had the bright idea to build a fire under the water tank to thaw the water. The tank was built on crossties that had been soaked in creosote. It did not take much for them to catch on fire, and that was the end of the water tank. It was never rebuilt. It was also the end of the local boys' swimming hole. The boys climb the tower to swim in the tank. If I had been around in those days, I would have been right there swimming in that tank. It was about that time the modern diesel engines were being put into service. The trains picked up and drop off mail for the Graysville community. Back in the day, trains going north dropped off mail and the trains going south dropped off mail. We went to the post office twice a day to get mail. After the depot was torn down, it was not an easy task to get the mail delivered. The mail was hung on a tall flagpole beside the tracks. The train whizzed by and a man with a hook snatched the mail sack off the pole. The incoming mailbag was tossed off the train. The postmaster had to walk up and down the railroad tracks until the bag was spotted on the tracks or in the weeds. Today a large mail truck delivers the mail to the post office and picks up out going mail. Back in the day, the old men hung around the depot just as they did the general store in later years after the depot was gone.

Mr. Gray built several cabins on the hillside above the springs. He built them for his children to vacation in during the summer. Many people in Graysville lived in the cabins throughout the years. Mr. Gray must have been the planter of pecan trees in Graysville. Almost every house has a pecan tree in the yard. I suppose the squirrels planted a few trees through the years.

In 1863 during the civil war, Sherman's wrath came down hard on Mr. Gray's businesses. His soldiers destroyed most of them. The furniture factory made gunstocks, cedar buckets and other items for the Confederate army. Many of the Graysville residents left Graysville for a while when the Union army came through burning almost everything. After the war, Mr. Gray worked to rebuild the railroad and restore his businesses. The gristmill was built in 1849 and was re-built after it was burned by the Union soldiers. Mr. Gray continued to work rebuilding bridges and railroads that had been destroyed during the war. Mr. Gray lived in Graysville until he died November 17, 1878. He is buried in the Graysville cemetery. My brother Bill likes to tell people that he was born about seventy years later on the same date that Mr. Gray died.

John D. Gray 1808 - 1878
Founding Father of Graysville, GA

THE CIVIL WAR

Graysville is rich in civil war history. People with metal detectors have found mini balls, belt buckles and other items all around Graysville. A little more than one hundred and fifty years ago, our country came face-to-face with an issue of equality and liberty for all citizens. It was the beginning of the Civil War. In my opinion, it was the worst thing that has ever happened in our country. It was a needless waste of life, and I still do not understand why problems could not have been solved without going to war. Blood was shed by American soldiers all over the North and South. It was brother against brother and father against son causing many families members to be split apart. Some fought for the North, and others fought for the South. It tore apart families, and reuniting after the war did not come easily. Peace finally came after four long years of dreadful war. However, there was not much peace in the hearts of most American people, especially the ones living in the war-torn states. They were filled with hatred for all their losses and what they had endured during those terrible years.

After the battle of Missionary Ridge, General Bragg's Confederate Army retreated towards Graysville on their way to Dalton, Georgia. Brig. General Cleburne's Brigade was the last group to leave Missionary Ridge. They were holding the rear guard, so General Bragg could get a head start. Both General Sherman and General Joseph Hooker tried to find the whereabouts of the Confederate forces. They pursued them in the direction of Graysville to try intercepting them. Around 10p.m. on November 26, 1863, General Cleburne's army arrived in Graysville on the West bank of the Chickamauga Creek. At this point the creek had to be forded. It was waist deep and the night was freezing cold. He postponed crossing until morning. In the early morning hours he received word to move to Ringgold Gap and hold back the Union Army at all cost. In their rush to leave the Confederates tried to start a fire on the bridge to slow down the Union Army, but they arrived in time to extinguish it and save the bridge. Shots were fired and many skirmishes were fought nearby. A few of the straggling Confederate soldiers were captured. General Cleburne's Army waited at Ringgold Gap for the Union soldiers. He felt it was a death trap since the Union Army out numbered him three to one. However, he was able to hold then back giving General Bragg time to get his army and supplies safely to Dalton, Georgia. Also at this same time, Stewart's Division and the Vanguard of Hooker's army were in battle at Concord. The battle started in the evening and lasted until the next morning ending in Graysville.

The next morning Graysville was full of Union soldiers and was in Federal hands. General Grant joined General Sherman along with a few thousand soldiers, and they camped a few days in Graysville. When they left Graysville, Sherman gave orders to his men to destroy all things connected with the railroad. They destroyed all of Mr. Gray's businesses. They also raided the gristmill taking all the flour and cornmeal to feed the soldiers and then burned the mill. Graysville was a thriving little village until the war broke out and Sherman came marching through. He burned almost everything, and Mr. Gray was never able to build Graysville back to the way it was before the war. After the battle at Ringgold Gap, General Grant ordered the railroad destroyed all the way back to Graysville. Everywhere Sherman passed on his march to the sea, he burned and destroyed everything. He left behind such a wasteland that most people had nothing to return to afterwards.

I have been told that a cannon was rolled into the creek near the bridge. If this is true, I would love for it to be retrieved from its long water grave.

The Ooltewah-Ringgold Road is straight as an arrow and goes from Ringgold, Georgia all the way to Georgetown, Tennessee, and beyond. A section of the road between Ringgold and East Brainerd Road is called Rabbit Valley or Pleasant Valley. These names are so unique. Pleasant Valley was formerly known as Rabbit Valley. Apparently, there were many rabbits in the area. Later, the people wanted a more pleasing name and changed the name to Pleasant Valley. The railroad runs parallel to the road. It is along this stretch of railroad, just a short distance from Ringgold, where The General train was captured during the civil war. On April 12,

1862, Andrew's Raiders, a group of Northern soldiers, highjacked The General. They captured The General early in the morning at Big Shanty when the crew and passengers stopped to eat breakfast. Big Shanty is now Kennesaw, Georgia. They headed north to Chattanooga on the Western and Atlantic Railroad that Mr. Gray built. The railroad ran from Atlanta, Georgia to Chattanooga, Tennessee. Their goal was to cut telegraph wires to prevent stations further north from receiving a message that the train had been stolen. The raiders job was to destroy the bridges, tunnels and telegraph lines and tear up tracks to prevent reinforcement coming from Atlanta. If successful, this would prevent the much-needed supplies from getting to the Confederate forces in Chattanooga. Andrews chose Big Shanty to steal the General because Big Shanty didn't have a telegraph. Someone would have to ride to Marietta to get the word out that the train had been stolen. It would give him time enough to make his escape and cut wires north of Big Shanty. The raiders unhitched the passenger cars and quickly left the station. They tried to do damage along the way, but were not as successful as they planned. The Texas arrived in Big Shanty as the General was leaving. They had no place to turn around so they ran backwards up the track after the General. The General passed the Catoosa on a side track. The Catoosa found out what was happening and joined in behind the Texas. The chase was on until around 1:00p.m. when The General ran out of wood and water and came to a halt about two miles north of Ringgold, Georgia. The chase lasted about seven hours and ended in failure. Andrew's Raiders scattered out into the country side. Fortunately, the Texas and Catoosa arrived in time to capture most of them. On June 6, 1862, Andrews and eight of the raiders were tried as spies and eventually hanged in Atlanta. Andrews and the eight along with others from the mission are buried in Section H of the Chattanooga National Cemetery. They are located in the Section H area where there is a monument, which consist of a granite pedestal topped with a bronze replica of "The General."

During this time in history, trains were given names, and later names were changed to numbers. The General was given the number three because it was the third oldest steam engine running at that time.

Today The General is preserved at the Southern Museum of Civil War and Locomotive History in Kennesaw, Georgia, which is listed on the National Register of Historic Places. The General was on display in several places before it came to Chattanooga in 1901. It was on display at the Chattanooga Depot for over fifty years. In the mid sixties, the state of Georgia wanted to reclaim the General and move it back to Kennesaw where the chase began. Georgia felt that it rightly belonged to them. Since it had been in Chattanooga for so long, Chattanooga felt that is where it belonged. In 1967, Kennesaw wanted to borrow the General to display and use for a fundraiser. Mayor Ralph Kelley, along with other politicians, felt that Georgia was trying to steal The General, and they would never let it come back to Chattanooga. Mayor Kelley and friends stood in the middle of the tracks and tried to block The General from being moved. This brought about lawsuits filed against the L&N concerning custody of The General. This was a long battle that went all the way to the Supreme Court. The Supreme Court refused to hear the case. A lower court eventually ruled in favor of the L&N Railroad. In February 1972, Georgia became the new home for The General, and the engine was moved to Kennesaw where it is still on display today. Most all Chattanoogans were sad to see The General leave.

The General

Civil War Canon

THE BLACKFORD-
GRAY HOUSE

The Blackford-Gray house is what we today call the Graysville house. It is a big, two-story, Victorian style house. Most people think that John D. Gray built the house, but it was built by Dr. Blackford sometime in the 1870s or 1880s. Dr. Blackford was a surgeon in the civil war. Charles Arthur Gray and John Gray, sons of Robert Gray, bought the house from Dr. Blackford in 1916. John D. Gray's son, Arthur Henry Gray, married Cora Linthicum from Ringgold, Georgia. They had a daughter named Nell. Arthur died in 1885 about three or four years after they were married. A few years later, Cora married Charlie Arthur Gray, who was the son of Robert Gray. I guess that is what is called keeping it in the family. Ms. Eaves' great-grandfather, Robert, never lived in the Graysville house and neither did John D. Gray. Nell married Alonzo Weathers, and they lived for a short period of time with Charlie Gray. People say they never heard Alonzo call Nell by her name. He always called her Precious. There was a small white house on the corner of the Gray property where Mr. Gray lived in later years. I remember seeing Mr. Gray in the mornings when riding to school on the bus. He would be sitting at the table eating breakfast and reading the paper. I always looked for him every morning and wondered what he was eating and why he got up so early.

The Graysville house has been sold many times since Mr. Gray bought it back in 1916. The Weathers lived in the house and after they were gone, the Bennetts bought the house. They lived there many years and sold it to Jack Lingerfelt. It has changed ownership several times since the Lingerfelts sold the house. One couple that bought the house turned it into a restaurant and named it the Graysville House. That is why today we still call it the Graysville house.

THE 1900S

Around the turn of the century, there was not much for people to do except work hard all week and go to church on Sundays. It was a period when they had to endure hard times, the coming great depression and two world wars. Even though times were tough, that period of time produced the greatest generation. They endured hardships, but they still had hopes and dreams that set an example for their children. With their determination and strong backs, they built this country.

Back then, they went to bed early and got up early. The girls helped their mothers with the cooking and household chores. If they did not have a well, they had to carry water from the springs to cook, clean house, wash clothes and bath. There was not much to do except visit with each other. Sometimes they ate lunch or shared the evening meal together. Sewing and quilting was something that was mastered by all the females. Church was an important part of their lives.

Some black families named Church lived on the hill near where the Postons now live. They were probably the descendents of the Church family slaves. The women carried baskets on their heads, and that really fascinated the young people. Sometimes the blacks had bar-b-ques, and the young people sneaked around and watch them. Watching the black people and church suppers were probably the only entertainment they had back in the day.

The young girls got together and walked to church or sometimes rode in a wagon with someone. The girls visited each other often during the week. They liked to get together, play games and sing. One thing they liked to do was sit on the steps in the sunshine on a cold winter day and crack hickory nuts. On cold winter evenings, they sat by the fire and ate peanuts, popcorn, hickory nuts and pecans. Those lucky enough to have a birthday during warm weather liked to have their birthday dinners at the springs.

A watermelon was usually floating around in the springs getting icy cold. It was a nice treat for a hot summer day.

Dr Dalton was the doctor in Graysville. Older people in Graysville remember him as being a good doctor. The world wide influenza epidemic of 1918 - 1920 killed millions of people. Dr. Dalton was credited for saving many lives during the flu epidemic that spread throughout Graysville and surrounding areas. Back in the 1800s it didn't take much to qualify to be a doctor. About all it took to qualify to be a doctor was a bottle of quinine, castor oil and a board to tape a broken bone to. Dr. Dalton must have gotten a good medical education to have known how to cure so many people with the influenza and deliver all those Graysville babies. Dr. Dalton's daughter Cecil was a real character. She usually carried a big stick everywhere she went. She was always joking and talking silly stuff. Once when the Graysville Methodist Women were going to be on a tv show, "Lunch and Fun" Cecil wanted to go. Some of the ladies thought that she might be an embarrassment because they had no idea what she might say. As it turned out, she was dressed nice and was as polite as all the other ladies. She liked to go visit people in the community every day. Hardly a day passed that she did not stop by our house. Cecil worked at the Graysville post office in her young days. At one time when she was postmaster the post office was in the front foyer of the Dalton house. After she retired, Peggy Swanson took her place and worked there until she retired. Many have come and gone since Peggy's retirement.

Some of the other early families that lived in Graysville were the Browns, parents of Pete and Bud. Their house was built sometime in the 1880s. The Simpson (Highpockets) house was built in the 1890s. The Reavely house was also built in the late 1860s. The Ward house is the only pre-Civil War house that is left standing. People still live in the other houses, except for the Brown house which is uninhabitable. The Dalton-Bynum house was built in the late 1860s. It was in a state of deterioration; however, Jack and Carolyn Towns took on the task of restoring the house. They succeeded, and restored it back to its original style. It is now a beautiful house reclaiming its glory from the days when it was first built. Jack and

Carolyn purchased the Fuller property and are clearing out the over-grown trees and weeds. The lake can be seen now, and it is going to be beautiful once again the way it was when Catherine lived there. Thanks Carolyn and Jack for helping to restore Graysville back to the good ole days.

FRED VAUGHAN

In the early 1900s, a family by the name of Vaughan lived in Graysville. They had a huge three-story house at the end of Graysville just as the road made a curve to go down the holler road as we called it back then. The road is now named Swanson Road. It goes from Graysville to Ooltewah-Ringgold Road also known as Rabbit Valley Road. In the late 1920s after Fred and his wife separated, he moved back to Graysville and lived with his mother. Fred had three children, two boys and a girl, which moved to New York with their mother. After a couple of years, their mother brought them to Graysville to visit their father and grandmother. Fred and his wife left together, but she did not come back with him, so the three children ended up living with him. They never saw their mother again. After a short time, they moved to one of the cabins that Mr. Gray built on a hillside at the springs. Fred did not know how to cook, and the little girl was too young; therefore, their food was scarce and ill prepared. Once he cooked a big batch of turnip greens in a lard can that had lead soldering. They were all poisoned and became so sick with a case of the trots that they thought they were going to die. Fred had a violent temper, and most everyone seemed to be afraid of him. He always carried a gun and thought that he was the local law since he was the Justice of the Peace, Notary Public, Fish and Game Warden and a Judge. He was not a judge, but he gave everyone the impression that he was one. He also had a small jailhouse that held one person at a time. He received letters at the post office from Governor Talmadge addressed to Judge Vaughan. People wondered if he really was a judge; but when the Governor of the state of Georgia addressed him as Judge, then the people did not question it. He was good friends with the Governor and asked several of the Graysville girls to go to the governor's ball with him, but they all declined. It was rumored that he was a member of the Klu Klux Klan so that was a good reason for people to fear him. Some people liked him and though he was a "good ole boy." I guess it was best to be on his good side.

Fred was really hard on his children. Once he whipped his son Patty with a boat paddle. His son James hated him and could not wait until he was old enough to run away. The children had no social activity with other members of the community. Fred's discipline was so strict that they were not allowed to talk to people when they went to the store or post office. Fred did let his son James visit the Touchstones. For James this was the best time of his life. The Touchstones were hard workers and grew big vegetables gardens along with their farming. They always had plenty of good food, and it was a treat for James to eat with them. One of his favorite foods they cooked was cornbread. When James was about 15, he and his father had a huge fight, and he was afraid for his life. He ran down to the Gray's house at the other end of Graysville. They had befriended him in the past and were not afraid of his father. They took him in, fed and clothed him. About a week later, Fred came looking for him. The Grays heard that he was coming so they gave James a quarter and he ran out the back door to escape. Somehow, at his young age he traveled to Chattanooga and from there to many other places. He never came back to Graysville until his later years in life.

One good thing Fred did was develop the springs at the end of Graysville. He turned it into an amusement park and named it Edgewater Beach. He had a concession stand and sold soft drinks and snacks. He also had boats that he rented out for people to paddle around in the creek. There was a rope and a diving board from which the swimmers loved to jump or swing. One young boy dived into the water and never came up. Of course, he drowned. That was a terrible thing for the people to see when they finally found his body and pulled him out of the water. Edgewater Beach was well known in the forties and fifties. People came for miles to enjoy a day of picnicing and swimming at the springs. When TVA built Chickamauga Dam and backed up the water, it formed a beautiful lake. Most people that went to the springs started going to Chickamauga Lake to enjoy their day in the sun. It was a great place to swim, picnic and sunbath. It was also a new place to go, and finally people just stopped going to Edgewater Beach. For a while in the early sixties, we girls would go to the springs to swim. After we stopped going nature took over, and the place became overgrown and forgotten until a few years ago when my brother brought it back to life. He cleaned out all the wild growing trees and brush. It again became a peaceful and beautiful place to visit. The trestle that passes over the creek at Edgewater Beach is a marvel of engineering that Mr. Gray accomplished. I suppose the Chruch Brothers cut and set the stones. It is probably one of the oldest trestles still being used by the railroad today.

This is our history lesson for now.

Clyde, Fred, James Madison, Spiere and Martha Vaughan
Kate Vaughan seated on steps.

The Vaughan House

STORIES

GOING BACK
TO GRAY'S ISLAND

Those of you, who read my book Gray's Island Where the Creek Bends, know how I like to reminisce about Graysville. After stirring up all those old, almost forgotten memories, I could not get Gray's Island off my mind. I decided that I had to see it just one more time. By the Grace of God, my desires were fulfilled.

It was in the late fall of 2014 after most of the leaves had fallen that I went back to Gray's Island. My brother Bill told me that he had found a trail that led back to the island. I cannot say how excited I was to think about going to see my favorite childhood playground. Our friend Cotton spends much of his time camping and rambling around in the woods. He also is a great lover of Graysville and has lived there most of his life. We asked him if he wanted to go with us, and he was ready to hit the trail. It was a beautiful autumn day. Once we started our hike, I didn't know if I would be able to make it all the way with my bad knees, but the desire to see Gray's Island was so strong it kept me going. We parked at the church and walked across the railroad tracks. First, we came to the spot where the old school house used to be. It burned a few years ago. It was very sad to walk around the grounds where the building once stood. We turned off the trail and walked a few short steps in the direction of where our little house used to be. It was like opening a door to the past. I don't know what happened to the house. Maybe it burned or was washed away by the creek. As I stood there remembering, my knees were cracking and popping as if they were going to break, my back was aching, and I was out of breath. With arthritis in my knees, I cannot walk very far the way I used to. Since I spend so much of my time indoors now, I did not realize how estranged from the outdoors I had become. I looked for the spot where I thought the house would have been and the big rock I fell over one night and cut my knee open. I looked at the area where I thought HighPockets' cornfield would have been. I imagined the dirt road that ran along side the cornfield and over the railroad tracks. I suddenly realized that the guys were going off and leaving me. I could have stayed there another hour just looking and remembering, but I knew that I had to push on. Once I got down to the creek, I would worry about how I was going to make it back to the car. Nothing looked the same. I was petty much disoriented once we started on the trail to the creek. I looked for the crabapple tree but did not see it. I could not find the spot where I turned off the trail to go jump off the diving board. We kept walking along the trail until suddenly the creek appeared. I could not believe my eyes. The island was almost completely gone. Only a few feet of gravel remained at the water's edge, and the rest was over grown with scrubby trees and underbrush. The bend in the creek was still there; finally, something I remembered. However, the big rocks that made the swift water had washed on down the creek. I could still see them under the pristine clear water. In my mind's eye, I could see all us children out there swimming around. Our little heads were bobbing up and down, and we were laughing and having so much fun. I could just picture us playing church and baptizing each other. Delores was the best baptizer. She would slap her hand over our mouth and nose; and with her other hand on our back, she dunked us down into the water. Sometimes just for the heck of it, she held us under a few seconds too long, and we came up out of the water kicking, splashing and screaming. Any onlookers might have thought we were filled with the Holy Ghost. We always got out of the water when the church people came to the creek for a baptizing. Our parents told us they had better not hear of us staying in the water during a baptizing. We certainly would have received a butt bustin if we had stayed in the water. Fortunately, we all had the good sense to do the right thing and always got out of the water and move as far away as possible. I suppose watching those scenes gave us the idea to baptize each other. I guess we never thought that baptizing each other might have been sacrilegious. Of course, I imagined the dreadful Fryar boys and Pig Plemons chasing us around the island. I could see these scenes almost as if they were really happening. I remembered in the fall that I would make one last trip to the creek by myself. I sat on the creek bank watching the leaves float by like little boats heading down the creek to the Tennessee River. Just as it is today, I remembered that the water was smooth as a pane of glass and the leaves were floating down stream. The clouds and blue sky reflected in the water painted a lovely picture that has been forever engraved in my mind. Actually, the creek and what was left of the island looked quite ghostly. It was heartbreaking to see what nature's floods had done to my world of childhood memories. Time washed away my island, but it did not wash away my memories.

THE FRYARS

Bill and Dixie Fryar were no strangers to Graysville. They both grew up in East Brainerd just across the Tennessee, Georgia state line. When Bill and Dixie were young, they along with a group of other teens used to walk down to Edgewater Beach. One day when they first started dating, they were at the springs when Dixie decided to smoke a cigarette. Back in the day, it was quite a promiscuous thing for a girl to smoke. The next day Bill walked all the way back to the springs to find the cigarette butt she had thrown down on the ground. That must have been when Bill decided he was in love and that one day Dixie would be his wife.

After Bill and Dixie married and started a family, they moved to Graysville. When they moved into the old school house in 1953, their son Dale was in the hospital. He had recovered from polio but still needed surgery on his legs. He wore braces on his legs for several months. In later years, the family teased Dale that they were trying to move off and leave him, but somehow he found them. The Fryars were the newcomers in the community. They were a handsome family. Glenda was a beautiful little girl, and the boys were all very good looking. Most all the girls in Graysville had a crush on the boys. They were envious of me because I lived next door to them. Dickie was such a mean rascal when he was young. I do not know how he turned out to be so nice after he grew up. Charles was always rather quite and did not get into as much mischief as Dickie. The Fryars bought the old school house and turned it into a home. That was an exciting time watching them work on the building. The old school house had three extremely large rooms, and they converted two of them into their living quarters. The third room where I spent my first three years of school was used as a garage. Bill had the largest garage and workshop, and he was probably the envy of all the men who knew him. Dale said that they were invited to Highpockets' house for a welcome-to-the-neighborhood dinner. He said they had opossum (I just say possum). Maybe they were just teasing him about what they were eating; but he swears that it really was possum, and he did not take the first bite.

We got our first television from Bill. It was his hobby to work on televisions and we were so grateful that he was kind enough to get us a good used one. We loved watching Mickey Mouse Club, Lassie, Daniel Boone, Gun Smoke and many other shows. Those innocent days were probably the best time of our lives.

The older boys in Graysville were always fighting about something. They really slugged out their disagreements. When we first moved to Graysville, my brothers were always coming home with black eyes, puffed up lips and bruises all over their bodies. They were always getting beat up until they were finally accepted into the neighborhood. The same thing happened to the Fryar boys. Of course, my brother Leon and his friend Allen (Unk) Harwood decided to check out Charles and Dickie to see how tough they were. They were punching each other in the stomach. According to their size, Leon and Charles were paired off, and Dickie and Unk were paired off. They were using each other for a punching bag. Dickie being the meanest punched Unk in the side and broke a rib. He says he really didn't mean to do it, but knowing Dickie he probably decided to end this contest and let them know that the Fryar boys were not a couple of wimps.

The Fryar boys and their friends also liked to play tricks on passing cars. Once they had the idea to tie a string onto a pocketbook, put it in the road, and then hide in the weeds to quickly pull it away when a car stopped. The boys were down the road somewhere around the hippo branch when they decided to play this trick on passing cars. Dickie ran home, rushed into the house, and grabbed his mom's brand new pocketbook. When they put it in the road, the first car that came by ran over it and smashed it flat. The driver of the car was non-other than my brother Leon. He had played that game himself so he knew what was going on. They pulled and twisted the pocketbook trying to get it back into shape, but had no such luck. The boys were in a lot of trouble over that prank. I guess that was a game played by many young boys across this great land.

Mr. Fryar bought a beautiful, shinny 1951 Chrysler car. It was one of the hottest days of the summer, and Mrs. Fryar decided to wash the car. She splashed a big bucket of cold water on the back window, and the glass cracked with lines like a roadmap. That evening when Mr. Fryar came home from work he said, "Dixie, what in the hell have you done!"

Mr. Fryar had a big flatbed truck. In the summer, Mrs. Fryar liked to take mom and all the children somewhere out in the boonies to pick blackberries. She always took us down a road that had lots of hills one after the other. She would go fast, and we bounced around in that old truck as if we were on a roller coaster. With all that bouncing around, we sure needed some seatbelts. It was hot, and the briars purposely seemed to reach out and scratch us when we tried to pick the berries. After a short time of being stuck by briars, we children were ready to go home. When we got back home, it was a trip to the creek to wash off the ticks, chiggers and other dirt we picked up out in the wild. Mom made a blackberry cobbler and jelly with the berries. We could hardly wait to dive into the pie.

Mrs. Fryar was a very brave and adventurous woman. She decided that she wanted to be on Queen for a Day. That was a radio and television program back in the fifties. She wrote a letter about her hard times and was accepted as a candidate. She was brave, got on that big plane, and flew to Chicago. She took Dale and Glenda with her. We were all in awe of her making the trip. No one from Graysville had ever been on a plane except for the boys who had been in service. The show was about whoever told the saddest and neediest story would be the winner. Her story was that she had four children. Her youngest son Dale had polio and almost died. He had many surgeries and wore braces on his legs. It was very difficult for him to walk. Of course, there were lots of doctor and hospital bills to be paid. Well, what do you know----She won! She was queen for a day and received many prizes. The only thing I remember is a big stuffed chair that she sat in the living room. The host of the show was infatuated with Glenda's sweet, little southern accent. He kept asking her questions just to hear her talk. During the show, he asked her if she had any pets. She told him that she had a pig and his name was Porky. At school, the principle brought in a radio so we could hear the program. It was awesome to hear her tiny voice travel hundreds of miles through the airwaves to our classroom. It was not so lucky for Porky. That winter when the weather turned cold Porky was sacrificed for the family table. My mom helped with processing the poor little guy. Of course, she brought home some pork that we did not want to eat. I guess hunger over took our loyalty to Porky because when the aroma of frying ham floated through the house we could not stay away from the table. We just bowed our head and said, "Thank you Porky for your sacrifice."

For some reason, one day when my sister Patsy, my brother Billy and I were playing with Dale and Glenda we got into an argument. This was something that happened almost daily, but it was never long before we were playing again. We were playing in a little barn between our house and the Fryar's house. I don't remember why, but I was mad at all of them. I broke off a nice big switch and chased them up the ladder to the loft of the barn. The loft was not a very large space. There was only one way up and one way down, and I was the keeper of the ladder. As I chased them up the ladder, I switched their legs. When they got to the top, I would not let them back down. When they tried to come down the ladder, I switched their legs again, and they quickly climb back up to the loft. I must have appointed myself the boss since I was the oldest. Finally, I had to let them down after we heard Mrs. Fryar call Dale and Glenda to come home. They were finally able to escape from being held captive in my barn-loft prison. I knew they would go home and tell on me, so I ran. Today, I guess one would call me a bully.

I was fourteen years old the last time I played with my dolls. I did not really care about playing with them anymore, but my younger sister Patsy wanted me to play dolls with her. She and I were sitting in the yard beside the house playing when suddenly up from the creek bank and around the back of the house came Dickie and one of his friends. When he saw me playing with the dolls, he pointed his finger at me and laughed. I felt so embarrassed that I never played with my dolls again. I do still have those two dolls after all these years. A few years earlier, I was playing dolls with Glenda in her front yard. She was playing with her new doll that she had gotten when her mom was on Queen for a Day. I was playing with a paper doll. For some reason, I guess it was jealously, I picked up her doll and sat it in a mud puddle and said, "Oh look, she wet he pants." She picked up my paper doll and smashed it in the puddle. She ran in the house crying, and I ran home.

One time Rebecca and Dickie got into a fight on the school bus. Dickie was sitting behind Rebecca's sister Delores, and he pulled her hair. Delores told him to stop, but he kept on. Rebecca jumped in the middle to protect her sister. She and Dickie had a heated argument. Dickie called her a half-breed, and Rebecca beat the tar out of him. Of course, the fight ended up in the principal's office, and Rebecca had to write a paper about good citizenship and not fighting on the bus. I don't remember what kind of punishment Dickie got. Rebecca was small, but she was tough as any of the guys. After that fight, nobody messed with Rebecca. We all respected her and did not want to get on her bad side. Just as Rebecca was the toughest girl in Graysville, Buddy Graham was the toughest boy. When the gang saw Buddy coming, they all stepped aside and gave him the right-of-way. I guess Dickie hanging out with Buddy is where he learned a lot of his meanness. It was just dumb luck that kept Dickie out of a lot of trouble.

Mrs. Fryar was always very nice to us children, but Mr. Fryar was a grouch. When he came home from work in the evening, we knew it was time to clear out of his way. He bought a bird dog to train for hunting. The dog's name was Gypsy. He taught Gypsy how to point. We thought seeing the dog point was so funny. Of course, it wasn't long before we learned how to make him point. We had a lot of fun playing with the dog until Mr. Fryar caught us making him point. He was so angry and yelled at us to stop because making the dog point would keep him from being a good hunting dog. Dale had a little blonde cocker spaniel dog named Ike. One time Mr. Fryar took his dog Gypsy bird hunting. He also took Dale and his dog Ike along with him. Ike followed along in Gypsy's footsteps and pointed just like he did. Mr. Fryar whipped Ike for joining in the hunt and pointing. When they got back home, Mr. Fryar tied Gypsy on a rope and went inside. Dale got a mimosa tree branch and whipped Gypsy. Mr. Fryar caught him and gave Dale a licking with the mimosa branch. I was too young to know anything about politics back then, but this dog named after President Eisenhower should have told me they were republicans. It is no wonder Dickie and I didn't get along since he grew up to be a republican, and I became a democrat. I do not remember what happened to Gypsy, but he was not around for very long. They also had a billygoat. It usually roamed around the yard. Sometimes he came down to our house, and we always ran inside. He would chase us and give us a butt if he got close enough. We were very afraid of him. That goat ate everything that was in front of him. He even chewed the paper off tin cans. I guess that is where the old saying came from that goats will even eat tin cans. The goat wasn't around for long either, and we were glad when the goat one day disappeared.

From left to right: Dick, Dale, Charles, Glenda & Shirley

PETE AND BUD BROWN

Pete and Bud owned the Graysville Mercantile Store. Mr. and Mrs. Weathers had the store before them. Pete and Bud built a new store sometime in 1953 or 1954. They had several antiques in the store. One was an old brass cash register, which they sold for a price they couldn't refuse. There was also an old authentic 1900s thread box, which was always filled with all different colors of thread. They gave credit to regular customers they trusted. They had a little book that they recorded sales in, and at the end of the week customers came in to settle up their bill. Those crisp, white aprons they wore were ironed smooth as silk by my mom. The store was always the heart of Graysville. This was the place to hear all the local news and gossip. The post office was the next place to find out what was happening in the neighborhood. The Catoosa County politicians always paid a visit and hung around the store during election times. It was a good way to meet with the people, pass out their literature and ask for votes. Pete often said that if the politicians didn't visit his store they would not get elected. When the store closed sometime before 1999, it seems like the community just died. Many of the young people had moved from Graysville; therefore, not many people were left after the older generation had passed away.

It was a sad day when the store closed. Pete and Bud dedicated many years of their life to the store and community. Before the big chain supermarkets were built, most communities had a general store where people bought their groceries and supplies. Pete and Bud not only stocked the store with food, but also had just about anything one might need. A few weeks before Christmas, the store smelled of fresh apples and oranges. There was a big antique wood and glass candy case that was loaded with all kinds of Christmas candies. My favorite was the pink, white, yellow or chocolate covered coconut balls. There was also a candy that was chocolate covered drops with a cream filling. They were delicious and; of course, there was a lot of peppermint sticks and assorted hard candies. It was a great time to go to the store and have your senses filled with the sweet aroma of Christmas. These scenes and smells have not faded from my memory. Actually, these candies can still be bought today, but they are just not as good as the ones we had back then.

Pete and Bud were great humanitarians. They helped more people than anyone knows. On Saturday evening, they gave the produce that would not keep over the weekend to a family in need. All the young children loved Pete and Bud. The children gave them their school pictures, and they taped them on a space near the cash register. It was fun for the children to go into the store and see their pictures taped to the wall. One day when my son was four years old, he was looking at a box of Premium crackers on a shelf. He told Bud that the Ms were upside down Ws. Bud asked him what each letter was in the word premium, and Richard told him. Afterwards, Bud asked him what it spelled and Richard said, "Crackers." Bud was amazed that he knew the alphabet at age four. Today most children know the alphabet by the time they can talk.

My brother Leon worked for Pete and Bud for several years. He saved up enough money to buy a nice bicycle. Sometimes he used the bicycle to deliver groceries. He rode his bike home for lunch every day. He always brought with him a quart of buttermilk and a small box of soda crackers. Sometimes he brought cheese to go with the crackers. We stood around watching him eat and wishing he would give us just one cracker, but he ate them all. I don't know why he even came home because he could have eaten at the store. Pete and Bud were teaching him how to cut meat and do other jobs in the store. Leon was offered a job by a local contractor to build houses. He took the job because he could make more money than Pete and Bud could pay him. He was a lot of help to them, and they were very disappointed to see him leave.

In their last years, Pete and Bud both became diabetic and lost their legs. Bud would ride up and down back street (Gray Street) in his wheel chair. He visited all the neighbors and really enjoyed being able to get outside. Once Bud's wheel chair brakes failed, and he just rolled right off the porch. That was a trip to the hospital.

One time the county did some roadwork on the streets in Graysville. After they were finished, Bud went out to inspect their work. He got his wheelchair stuck in the soft asphalt and could not get it out. A neighbor saw the situation he was in and came to help. She attached a chain from her car to his chair and pulled him out. Then she cleaned his wheels. That's the kind of neighbors who live in Graysville. They are always ready to lend a helping hand.

In 1947 or 1948 the decision was made to un-incorporate Graysville. The last mayor of Graysville was non-other than Pete Brown. However, through the years people still referred to him as the mayor.

Master's grocery was another grocery store near Graysville. When we moved to Graysville, my brothers would go to the store to get ice cream. They loved chocolate covered ice cream on a stick, which we call brown cows today. In Hawkinsville, they called the ice cream choc-cows, and when they asked Mr. Masters for a choc-cow, he did not know what they were talking about. He told them he did not have any. They would get so angry and knew that he had the choc-cows because they saw other people eating them. Finally, they figured out how to tell him what they wanted. I don't know if they had this problem at Pete and Bud's store, but I suppose they did if they asked for a choc-cow.

Sometimes the railroad parked train cars on a side-track in front of the store. We called them camp cars. The railroad crew stayed in them at night and worked on the tracks during the day. They were sometimes there for a few weeks. This brought in a lot of business for Pete and Bud. The crew had to be fed and what better place to get good food than at Pete and Bud's store. There was a cook that stayed in the camp cars during the day and had dinner ready for the crew when they came back in the evening. Other times they ate a lot of Pete and Bud's famous sandwiches. It was always interesting to see so many new faces in Graysville. However, sometimes it was good to see them leave.

CHATTANOOGA NEWS-FREE PRESS, SUNDAY, NOVEMBER 8, 1959

Old-Timey Store ... Coffee,

Caught by a local trapper last fall, this 41 pound, stuffed bob cat "has raised more than one newcomer's eyebrows" when they enter the Graysville Mercantile Store, owned by brothers Pete and Bud Brown. "I'd heard all my life that they were around here," Pete said, noting that the bob cat was trapped only about a mile from the store, "but this is the first one I ever saw."

Although Pete Brown wouldn't give away his "secret," local residents contend that something about their hand-cut meat makes it "taste better," exemplified in the fact that the brothers sell between 2,500 to 3,000 pounds per week. Here, he is shown in the well-stocked meat locker.

Pete and Bud Brown; photo Courtesy
of the Chattanooga Times Free Press

THE TOUCHSTONES

In 1933, Fred Vaughan married J. T. Touchstone and Lorene Jarrett in a boat in the middle of Chickamauga Creek. They thought that they were slipping off to get married. Fred paddled them up the creek for a short distance. After saying their vows, he pronounced them man and wife and paddled them back to Edgewater Beach. Someone let the cat out of the bag, and word got out about the wedding. When they came back down the creek, almost everyone in Graysville was standing on the creek bank waiting for them. After getting married, the Touchstones lived in one of Mr. Gray's cabins at the springs. Their daughter Marie was born in the cabin. Later they had moved across the creek by the time Tommy came along.

The Touchstones were all attractive people, especially the girls. Their black hair and brown eyes seemed to glow when they smiled. Dr. Dalton was the local doctor in Graysville. He delivered some of the Touchstone children. When younger brother Tommy was ready to enter the world, Mr. Touchstone walked to Graysville to get Dr. Dalton. They were in a hurry and wanted to take a short cut back across the creek. There was a place where the water was not very deep, and one could step on rocks and wade across. Later a swinging bridge was build near this spot. Dr. Dalton did not want to get his little black bag wet, so Mr. Touchstone carried him on his back across the creek. Fortunate for Mrs. Touchstone to have a doctor since Tommy entered the world weighing twelve pounds. He was her last child, and we don't have to wonder why. Many of the children born in Graysville were delivered by Dr. Dalton. Marie, and her brothers and sisters all swam and played in the creek, but they never jumped off the bridge. Marie said that her mother's brother jumped off the bridge and that the blood came up before he did. She doesn't remember what happened, but he did survive.

These are the memories of Marie Touchstone Wright, which she so graciously shared with me.

The following are memories written by Loreeta Touchstone Darling:

My fondest memories of growing up in Graysville until I was twelve years old was going swimming in the creek down below the dam. Marie, who was my first cousin on my dad's side and my aunt on mom's side always took Marsha, Cathy and myself swimming. Afterwards, we would go to Pete and Bud Brown's store for a coca cola and a candy bar. The cokes and candy were five cents each. That was the good old days!

Graysville was the greatest place to grow up. Everyone knew everyone, and we always felt safe there. We had to walk a mile around the creek road (Dug Road) to catch the school bus. My brother James and I, the Hammontrees, Marsha and Cathy Wright all walked together.

Our town had one fantastic store, which was Pete and Bud Browns, and a little rock building post office. I can remember as a child standing in front of the store watching the hobos on the trains when they passed by. Our house sat not too far from the tracks, and I can remember hobos coming to our house for something to eat. My mom would never let them into the house, but she would have them sit on our porch and give them food.

We went to New Liberty Baptist Church, and Frank Craton was our pastor. He and his family would sometimes come to eat at my Granny and Grandpa's house. Some of the good memories were of my family sitting around outside in the little cane bottom chairs and enjoying good food and good times. It was a common thing back then for the pastor to go home with church members for Sunday dinner.

In 1961 when I was ten and my brother was sixteen, we had a "horrible" thing happen in our family. My mom Bessie took her life. If it wasn't for family close by, I don't know what my dad, brothers and I would have done. When I was twelve, my dad re-married and we moved to Adairsville, Georgia. My brother went into the Navy. I really missed Graysville. In 1968 that same preacher, Frank Craton, married my husband and me. That was 46 years ago.

The following memories are from James H. Touchstone, Jr, who at age 82, 83 and now going on 91, could still remember this about his past.

I was around five or six years of age when we lived in a tenant house on Mrs. Heck's place. We lived there almost seven years. We then moved into a tenant house on Mrs. Sells' farm that joined Mrs. Heck's place. My dad bought a house and ten acres of land for $500.00. In 1946, he tore down the old house and built a new one. It was a white house across from Melvin and Marie Wright in Graysville, Georgia.

While on Mrs. Heck's farm, one summer we raised enough corn to fill 44 two-horse wagonloads plus cotton and vegetables. We would make large hills in the garden and bury enough sweet potatoes and turnips to last all winter. When I was in my late teens, papa paid me $1.50 per day to help on the farm. All my brothers were married and had moved off, so I was the only boy left at home. I thought I was rich.

My mom had chickens. What eggs we didn't use ourselves, we would take to Chattanooga in Mrs. Heck's Model-T Ford in exchange for sugar, flour and coffee. We would take large bags of corn to the grist mill, and he would take out so much corn in exchange for grinding our corn into cornmeal.

Nelson and J.T. picked enough cotton in one day that they were in the newspaper. One had picked over 300 pounds, and one had picked over 400 pounds of cotton.

One of my brothers (I believe Lloyd) could eat as many as ten biscuits at one meal. It probably took ten biscuits to fill him up after doing all that hard work. We always ate good.

When the twins, Nelson and Wilson, were four months old, mama's milk dried up. She was proud that the sweet potatoes were coming in because that is how she kept them alive.

Bessie and I lived with my sister Mildred until Edgar got out of the Army. That's where we had James. It cost $40.00 for his birth, and that was for a night's stay and a nurse to look after him at Dr Stevenson office in

Ringgold, Georgia. Lareeta was born there six years later, and by then the price had gone up to $60.00 for a birth. When I was born, a mid-wife helped deliver me, and I was told later that it cost $3.00 to deliver me.

We bought our first house in Roach Holler for $150.00. It had two rooms, a cistern for water, a toilet and a large lot. After my dad tore his house down and built a new one, we paid him $150.00 for one acre of land and the good wood lumber out of the house he had torn down. It also included his labor to build us a two-room house, which we later added on to. Bessie bought an additional acre for $60.00, which gave us two acres. My dad, Uncle Charlie Black, Mr. Rinehart, Mr. Freeman, and I built our house.

My dad loved to go fishing, and he also loved his chewing tobacco (Ole Brown's Mule). When I was a young boy and my dad (papa) would go to the store, I always looked for a brown bag sticking out of his pocket when he returned. If I saw one, that meant he had brought us home some candy.

When we were young, Mrs. Heck would come over at Christmas and give us each an envelope with a dollar in it. That was a lot of money back then.

THE POSTONS

Mac and Bobbie Poston moved to Graysville in 1947. They heard about Graysville from some men that Mac worked with and decided it might be a good place to live. They were a handsome couple and had six beautiful children. I guess Mac was determined to have a son. After five girls, a little boy finally came along. The doctor told Mac that he finally got a little boy, and Mac said, "Show me!" He was named McCracken, Jr. and is better known in Graysville as Ken. During that time people in Graysville had phones with a party line. They were on a party line with Mrs. Simpson. They were so excited and were on the phone all day calling everyone they knew to tell them they had a little boy. Finally, Mrs. Simpson was so annoyed that she called and told them to get off the phone. That little boy grew into a handsome and kind man. He studied law in college and became a locally famous attorney. My husband John calls him the Matlock of Ringgold, all in due respect, of course. Matlock is his favorite TV show. Since Ken gets so many high profile cases in the area he seems to fit the imagine of Matlock. He is a very brilliant and respected attorney. He is not like all the lawyer jokes we hear. He gives a lot of himself to the community and is always ready to help his fellow Graysvillians if they should need council.

Mary Nell (Bunny) was their first-born and is the same age as me. She was always extremely smart. She attended the University of Tennessee at Chattanooga and later became a college professor. Before retiring, she was the interim president of UTC for about a year. She set a good example for her younger siblings Carolyn, Jan, Katy, Nancy and McCracken, Jr. (Ken). Bunny set the bar high, but they all followed in her footsteps and got a good educated and held important jobs. I have always been very proud of Bunny and wished that I could have been as smart and pretty as she.

Once when I was a teenager, Carolyn wanted me to give her a perm. Her mother always talked about the Brock girl's pretty blonde hair. I had never

44

given anyone a perm before; but stupid like, I said that I would do it. It took forever to get her hair rolled. When I finally finished, her hair was fried and looked like it had been rolled on toothpicks. I was so embarrassed that I had ruined her hair. Just in case I never told you, Carolyn, I am saying it now, "I am so sorry."

There are three houses on Poston hill, and the Postons lived in the middle house for many years. They now live in the last house that was once the Methodist church parsonage. I suppose they always had to be on good behavior living next door to a minister. One time when the preacher parked his car and did not put it in gear, it rolled down the hill and hit a tree. The kids all ran down the hill to check out the car. Prowling around his car, they found a large bag of coins and were excited about the treasure they had found. It belonged to the preacher, so they had to give it back.

Carolyn and Jan were always getting into some kind of mischief. Once they slipped off from home and went down to Mrs. Simpsons who lived beside the post office. They picked all her daffodils. They didn't pick long enough stem, so they could put them in a vase. They just snapped off the blooms at the top. Mrs. Simpson was so angry that she called their mother complaining about what they had done. Another time they slipped off to the springs. They were playing when suddenly they came upon a big black snake. They started screaming and ran for home. As they were running, the sound of their voices traveled through the air, and Mrs. Poston though they had fallen in the creek and were being washed away.

One day Mac and Preacher Baker decided to go fishing. They paddled up the creek and found a good place to fish. After they had been fishing for a while, Preacher Baker said, "Mac, if you want to get that beer out from under your seat and drink it, I will smoke my cigar." Mac was so surprised that he knew about the beer all he could say was, "I didn't know you smoked." They both found out secrets about each other on that fishing trip.

Mrs. Poston said when they moved to Graysville that Pete and his family lived next door. She saw his wife Lee hanging out diapers and asked her, "how old is your baby?" Lee said, "The same age as yours." Mrs. Poston did not know that she and Lee were in the hospital at the same time. She had Jan on the same day that Lee had Trudy. Having so many girls, Mrs. Poston was always giving birthday parties. On Jan's birthday, Trudy always came and had her party with Jan. Trudy and Jan were best friends.

Once Ken was prowling around a train that had stopped in front of the store. When box cars were empty, the doors were often left open. Ken crawled up in a box car, and suddenly the train started moving. He did not know what to do. Finally, he was brave enough to jump. He was about half-way to Ringgold by then and had to walk all the way home. Writing these stories makes me think that those Poston kids were about as mischievous as the Fryar kids.

Mrs. Poston said that my mom was the first person who came to visit her when she moved to Graysville. She always talked about us having blond hair, and her children all had dark hair. I do not remember that visit since I was only around four or five years old. Mom and Mrs. Poston always liked each other. My mom was the best mom in the world. Now that she is gone Mrs. Poston is the best mom in the world. All moms are the best.

Thank you Mrs. Poston for being so kind to share your memories with me. You are a very special person.

CATHERINE FULLER

One day when Catherine Fuller's husband was driving through Graysville, he saw Mr. Graham putting up a for sale sign. Mr. Fuller stopped to look at the property. He bought it that very day. The Fullers were of the Lutheran faith, which was strange to us because everyone in Graysville was either Baptist or Methodist. Catherine loved her home, and she made it a beautiful place that filled the soul with good old Southern comfort. She wanted some white face cattle for the front grounds by the pond. She called it a lake. There was a spring at the bottom of the hill in the back of their house. The water from the spring made a stream that filled in a large area that formed the lake. A stream of water ran from the lake to the road, and that is what we called the Hippo Branch. She thought it would be so peaceful to look out and see the cattle grazing beside her lake. She bought three white face cows and put them in her front yard. That very night they were stolen. That was the end of her dream seeing cattle grazing in her front yard. After her cows were stolen she decided to raise Doberman pinchers. Nobody was about to steal one of them. Years ago, someone built a springhouse around the spring at the bottom of the hill. Before electricity, people put milk, butter and other items in the cold spring water to keep them cool. In the summer, Catherine liked to sit in the springhouse and read where it was nice and cool. The springhouse was a place of tranquility where she nurtured her soul with peace and strength.

Catherine had four children, two boys and two girls. Her son Jimmy loved to do repelling and rock climbing. He found a gun drawing that was carved into a rock on the hill behind their house. It was probably carved by one of the civil war soldiers when they were camped in Graysville. The whole family liked to climb around on the hillside, look at the gun drawing on the rock, and ponder over who might have drawn it. One of her daughters had a boyfriend that came to pick her up in a helicopter. We thought that was awesome to see it fly in and land in front of the house near the lake. In later years, Catherine started attending the Graysville United Methodist Church. She has been a devoted worker and fundraiser for the church. She is loved by all who know her.

LONG DISTANCE

Long Distance was another one of those nicknames. He was a very tall skinny man with a look that frightened all of us children. He had an evil grin and eyes that seemed to just pierce through our body. On my trips to the store, my fear of passing the cornfield and the hippo branch was nothing compared to meeting up with Long Distance. He never bothered me or any of the children, but that sly grin was very un-nerving. When meeting him I usually crossed the road to the other side and looked down at my feet so I would not have to speak to him. Thinking about him today, reminds me that he was sort of like the character (Boo) in the book "To Kill a Mocking Bird." I never knew his name, other than his nickname, "Long Distance." He had very short twin brothers that we called the Jerrys. I never knew their names either, or why we called both of them Jerrys. They were very short compared to Long Distance's height.

THE SELFS

Bill and Clara Self grew up in Graysville, married and had a large family. They lived on Hill Street. We always think of Graysville having just two streets, Front Street and Gray Street. There was another street on the side of the hill, and that is where the Selfs lived and where Pete Brown built a house. On Mother's Day, the church would give flowers to the women for certain things such as being the oldest mother, the youngest mother, or the mother with the most children present at church with her. Mrs. Self usually always won for having the most children present.

The Selfs had some Indian in them from generations back. Mrs. Self's mother was part Cherokee Indian. However, the genes were strong and their complexion looked as if they had a nice tan. They all had dark hair and brown eyes. I thought they were very pretty girls and wished that I looked like them. I always wanted to have dark hair and brown eyes. I did my best every summer by getting a nice brown suntan.

A few times Delores asked her mother if I could come home with her after church and eat dinner. Mrs. Self always cooked a big Sunday dinner with cake for dessert. It was always delicious. She was a very good cook and spent a few years cooking in the Graysville Elementary School cafeteria.

After graduating high school, I got a job at Davenport Hosiery Mill and rode to work with Mr. Self and his son Avery. I sat in the back seat and never said a word. I just listened to them talk about politics and Mr. Self saying that he was going to retire as soon as he turned sixty-five and not a day later. It was a few years later that Mr. Self built me a cage for my pet rabbit. One think I remember about Mr. Self, other than he was a very nice man, was that he loved turtles. They were one of his favorite foods. I think that he made turtle soup with them. It made me squirm when I saw him coming back from a fishing trip carrying a turtle. Years later, I was finally brave enough to taste turtle when we were vacationing on Grand Cayman Island. It tasted better than I expected.

The Self girls used to sing in church. There was Ann, Geneva, Dalphna, Rebecca and Delores. They did not always let Delores sing with them. They all had very pretty voices. The congregation always loved to hear them sing. I always wished that we Brock girls could sing in church, but none of us were blessed with any musical talent. Once, I was lying on the bed with my feet propped up on the wall and singing as loud as I could. My sisters were tired of hearing me and they told me to stop. I told them that I was practicing and was going to sing in church. They laughed and laughed at me. That ended my hopes of a singing career.

One summer Rebecca, Dalphna and Delores along with, Martha and Allen Harwood, went blackberry picking on Moody Hill. Moody Hill is another name for Scrapeshin Ridge behind their house. After they had each picked a nice pail of berries, they were ready to go home. On the way home Dalphna saw a green snake on the path. She screamed and threw her arms up in the air, knocking Allen's pail of berries out of his hands spilling them all over the ground. He was so upset about losing his berries that they all divided their berries and filled up his pail.

Rebecca and Delores used to catch rabbits in their rabbit gums. Their mother fried them up golden brown, and they had a delicious meal. When they caught a possum their dad took it to the foundry where he worked and sold it for two dollars. They always liked catching a possum because it gave them some spending money. I wonder if Leon every caught a possum in one of his rabbit gums.

Delores was my age, and she spent a lot of time with me swimming in the creek. Her sister Rebecca was a couple years older, so she was one of the lucky girls that got to go to Martha's house on Sunday. This was when Delores and I spent our time at the creek fighting with Pig Plemons and the Fryar boys.

THE SWANSONS

George Washington Swanson and his wife Gertrude moved to Graysville around 1938 or 1939. Most everyone in Graysville called Mr. Swanson G.W. The Swansons lived in Rabbit Valley on Ooltewah-Ringgold Road near the Tennessee state line before moving to Graysville. They lived in the house where the Grahams and Catherine Fuller lived until they built their house and sawmill. Their youngest daughter Martha was born in Graysville and her younger brother Bobby was born at Dr. Stevenson's clinic in Ringgold. The other children were born before they moved to Graysville. The Swansons had a large family. They moved in buying up every acre of land in and surrounding Graysville. Mr. Swanson needed all the land he could get to harvest the trees for his sawmill. Martha said, "She remembered hearing her family say they moved to Graysville to be closer to a school." The children had to walk to Ringgold to go to school, and that was a long walk for young children. Mr. Swanson built the sawmill, and that was probably one of the reasons they settled in Graysville. He also owned the old mill where people came to grind their corn into cornmeal. When Mr. Swanson bought the gristmill and land from Mr. Gray he was following in his footsteps to help Graysville grow. He hired several of the local men to work in his sawmill. He was also kind and helped some of his employees by providing them a place to live.

Martha and my sister Peggy were best friends from first grade until present day. All the girls Martha's age went to her house every Sunday. They tell stories of all the fun things they used to do. One trick they liked to play on passing cars was to fill a cornmeal bag with sawdust. They tied a string on the bag and put it on the side of the road. They hid in the weeds, and when a car stopped to pick up the bag of cornmeal they pulled it out of sight with the string. By the time the people got out of their car they could not find it. They also put the bag on the side of the road and watched people stop to pick it up thinking they had cornmeal only to get on down the road to find it was a bag of sawdust. They thought this trick was the funniest thing in the world. Just like the Fryar boys, I guess this game was played one way or another all across this great land.

Sometimes when the girls spent the night with Martha, her dad took them possum hunting. They rambled around out in the dark woods looking for possums. After a few times of being led around in the woods on cold winter or hot summer nights they decided that they had enough of possum hunting. Peggy always came home from Marthas telling about all the adventures they had and I was so mad because she would never let me go with her. However, in the summer I usually ended up having a good day getting to go swimming at Gray's Island.

Martha took piano lessons from Mrs. Frank who lived up the road from where we lived. Peggy liked to go with Martha to take her lessons. It cost fifty cents for a piano lesson. One day Martha decided that she did not want to go, so instead she bought a box of chocolate covered cherries with her fifty cents. She and Peggy sat on the side of the road and ate the whole box. This went on for a few weeks until one day a big thunder storm blew up and Martha's mother sent her brother Harlan to pick her up from her lesson. He went in to get her and Mrs. Frank said, "I have not seen Martha in about a month." Martha said that when she got home her mother gave her a good licking and from then on she took her lessons every week.

Hope Came with the Sunrise By: Patsy Simpson

As I recall my earliest memories of Graysville, I go back to when I was just a small child. My family lived in a tiny house that sat between Front Street and the railroad tracks and just about on the tracks. We used to enjoy watching the passenger train come through, and we would all run to look out the back door and wave at the passengers. The light inside that passenger train seemed so warm and the faces on the passengers did too. It seemed like they were really enjoying their train ride. No doubt, some of them were probably laughing at us and thinking, "just look at those country rednecks." We met some real characters when the hobos hopped off the trains that stopped by our house. Mother would fix them a sack lunch, which usually consisted of biscuits and whatever she could scrounge up. They were always grateful to get whatever she gave them.

My parents were Harold Richard Bynum and Nannie Lou Peterson-Bynum. Once my father told me the story of how his parents, Eugene Bynum and Cecil Dalton met, and I thought it was interesting. Eugene Bynum lived in Wichita, Kansas, and Cecil lived in Graysville, Georgia. Eugene rode the train through Graysville to deliver the mail to the Graysville post office depot. One beautiful spring morning as Eugene was hanging off the side of a train to put the mail bag out on the hook, he saw my grandmother Cecil as she was coming to collect the mail. He called to her and asked if she would marry him. She had never laid eyes on him before, but she agreed to marry him anyway. I guess that's what we refer to as "love at first sight." Cecil's father was Dr. John Dalton. I think it would've been nice to meet him. People have always spoken very highly of him. He practiced medicine during the time when one doctor had to treat a lot of different ailments; and sometimes instead of being paid with money, he would receive a few chickens or fresh eggs as his payment. Grandmother Cecil also had two brothers, John and Hunter Dalton. Hunter was a lawyer, and John was a drunk. Daddy always claimed that John killed his father

Eugene, but others told that Eugene died after he had been drinking some bad homemade whiskey with some other men at the Graysville springs.

Growing up in Graysville was nice. Generally, it was a quiet place with the springs in walking distance, so we could carry good fresh water to drink. One funny memory I have is something that happened one Halloween night. We didn't have indoor plumbing or a bathroom, so we had an old outhouse. One night a bunch of the young boys that lived around there came up and set our outhouse down on the railroad tracks while we were asleep. I don't know who had to go to the outhouse first the next morning, but I'm sure they were saying something like "Gotta go, gotta go, gotta go. Oh no, where will I go?" They were surprised to see that the outhouse was sitting on the tracks. Luckily, no trains came through that night, and we were able to get the outhouse back up the bank and to the pot hole before it was hit by a train.

Another memory I have was when mother gave birth to a new baby boy without any help from anyone else. She said she had a headache and felt terrible, so she sent my older brothers to the store for aspirins. My older sisters were in school. She had Francis and me sit on the couch and told us that she was going to lie down for awhile. She gave us strict orders to sit on that couch and not to move an inch until she got up. We knew we'd better listen and do as she said. While we were sitting there, we heard a weird noise that sounded like a cat. Francis said, "That old tomcat is after momma, so you'd better go check on her." I said, "Oh no! You're just trying to get me in trouble!" Then momma yelled, "Girls, go into the kitchen and get the scissors and matches." She told me to carry the scissors with the sharp edge pointed down toward the floor. We did as she said, and she had us sit on the couch again until she could get up. When she did get up we had a new baby brother, Melvin Dewayne! She put Melvin in a basket and carried him into the living room where we were sitting; she told us she had found him down on the railroad tracks. We were so excited about the baby. We wanted her to go back and look again to see if there were any more babies, one that might not cry so much! This will always remain fresh in my mind as if it only happened yesterday. Even thought she was having childbirth pains, she still was concerned about our safety and gave instructions about how to carry those scissors.

Shortly after the birth of our brother, we went to live with Mamaw and Papaw for a while because we were having a hard time with finances and keeping food on the table. My grandparents, Frank and Ruth Peterson, kept us from starving. The time spent with them was wonderful as I recall. They lived on a farm which belonged to someone else, and they took care of the animals in return for a place to stay. We helped feed the horses and the cows, along with the chickens and pigs. It was a nice, big farm with lots of pretty land for miles around. This is the same land where the producers filmed the movie "Water for Elephants" starring Reese Witherspoon. When we lived there, out back of the house there was a field of rabbit tobacco and blackberries growing everywhere. Papaw would pick the blackberries and wash them; and then after he added a little bit of sugar, he would sit my brother Lonnie on his knee and feed them to him. Lonnie was Papaw's favorite of us all.

There was a steep hill out to the side of our grandparents' house, and all of us kids would get a big piece of cardboard and slide down the hill. Oh, what fun! You never heard such squealing and laughing. We also got to decorate a Christmas tree when we stayed with them, and it was so pretty with sparkling icicles. At night the reflection of our beautiful Christmas tree showed in the window, which doubled its beauty. The Mashburns owned the farm, and late on Christmas Eve they sneaked in a little gift to make sure there was something for all us kids.

I have such pleasant memories of our time spent on the farm; it was a very happy time. One day we were able to move back to Graysville. We lived there in Graysville until our house burned down. The evening the house caught on fire momma was frying some chicken on the old woodstove when she noticed a flame up around the stovepipe and along the back wall. She screamed, "Get all the kids out. The house is on fire." Then she grabbed that big iron skillet of chicken off the stove and ran out the door with it. She wasn't going to let that chicken go to waste. I'm sure she probably had to wring that chicken's neck and pluck its feathers before getting to cook it, and she didn't want all that work to be done for nothing.

After the house burned, daddy built another house on that same property that was just a two-room shack with a dirt floor. It was after we moved into that house when the accident happened to my baby sister, MaryAnn. We were all at school that day except for MaryAnn and my older sister, Janie. Momma had gone with daddy to help him finish up a tree-cutting job that day. It was winter time, and there was a fire built in the wood stove. We didn't have a chimney, so somehow the wind blew down the stove pipe blowing fire out the bottom of the stove. MaryAnn was in front of the stove, and the fire blew out the bottom and caught her little dress on fire. Janie tried to put it out with her hands, but MaryAnn ended up with third-degree burns over a big portion of her small, one year-old body. She was rushed to the hospital; and that day when I came in from school, they were just bringing her back home. She was wrapped in white gauze from her head to her toes and looked like a mummy. I was so worried. She should've stayed at the hospital because that night she had to go back. This time they kept her for several weeks. We didn't see her again until a year or longer because the next time she left the hospital she was placed in a foster home. Momma went to court and fought to get her baby back. My parents had to prove they could provide for her as well as the rest of the family. Dad had to get a better house, so we moved to Chickamauga. When we finally got MaryAnn back, she didn't even know who we were. She didn't want to stay with us, and she had to learn who we were all over again.

I think about some of these things that happened when I was growing up, and I know that God was taking care of my family and me. There were times we were so hungry, but at those times God would send someone with food, many times delivered in boxes by people we didn't even know and just left on our door steps. He sent people to help at just the needed times.

This life is a journey from the time we are born until we leave here. Along life's path, there are going to be some bad things that happen and some good things. I try to look at the positive side of it all. It makes me think of the movie "Ole Yeller," which is a favorite of mine. There's a part in that movie that is special to me, and that is the part when the father comes home from his journey and goes upon the hill to comfort his son who has just buried the ole yeller dog. The father said, "Son, ever now and then for a reason no man can figure out, life will haul off and slam you against the ground so hard you think your insides are coming out. But it ain't all bad. There's some mighty fine things that comes along with it, and you've got to take the good along with the bad." It's so true for all of us.

One of the most wonderful memories I have as a child in Graysville is one of the good things of life, and that is I can remember my very first sunrise. A lot of people can't say that they remember the first time they really noticed a sunrise, but I can. I awoke one morning to brightness in my room. The brightness was actually what awakened me. I looked around and I saw bright streams of light filtering through my bedroom window. The entire room was filled with such brilliance. I scrambled upon my knees on the bed and placed my elbows on the windowsill, cupping my chin in my hands, and I looked out toward the Eastern sky. There it was, the most beautiful sunrise. My very first sunrise was so bright and beautiful, and it made me so happy. I'll always find happiness in the sunrise. With each new day we can have a fresh start; and if there's something that we failed with yesterday, we can try again to make it right today. I feel that God gave me that special sunrise that morning to put some light and happiness in my life. He wanted to let me know that He is the Maker and that I could always find hope in Him. It was as if He said, "Look, Patsy, what I created for you. If I can do all this, don't you know I can take care of you, too? Just look at the warmth and light I give to you and brightness to take the place of the dark things in your life." So whatever I have come through, good or bad, I know there is always hope. Every year now on Good Friday, I go up on the hill behind my house and watch the sunrise. I reflect on my journey through this life, the lives of my children and now the lives of my grandchildren. I pray for them, and I thank God for them. I thank Him for sending his Son Jesus to die on the cross for my sins. I thank Him for the hope I found in that first sunrise that He gave especially to me that beautiful morning so many years ago.

The Bible tells us in James 1:2-4 "count it all joy when you fall into trials, knowing the testing of your faith produces patience. But let patience have its perfect work, that you may be perfect and complete, lacking nothing."

This story was written for the book by Patsy. In her words she tells about her life growing up in Graysville. Patsy is a pretty girl and was probably the prettiest girl to ever live in Graysville. She is a special person, and I am glad she is my friend. Thank you, Patsy.

Patsy and Shirley

HIGHPOCKETS

Herb Simpson, alas Highpockets, was one of the old men that sat on the bench in front of the store when he wasn't planting or harvesting corn near our little house on the creek. I wish that I had some of Highpockets corn now. I would boil it and eat it right off the cob like a hungry beaver chewing down a young sapling tree to build himself dam. Most all of the men sitting around in front of the store spent their time whittling, chewing tobacco, spitting and talking politics. They liked to use cedar wood for their whittling. One of the men was Bob Simpson. He liked to whittle his piece of wood into a sharp point and stick the young boys as they walked by. Kenneth Childers was one of his favorites to punch with his sharp pointed stick. When I went to the store, I always hated to walk past the old men. I never looked at them. I was always looking down to be sure I did not step in the tobacco they spit all over the ground. Since I was usually always barefooted in the summer, I certainly did not want to step in that nasty tobacco spit.

Bob Simpson was a brother to Highpockets. He was also Mrs. Nell Robinson's brother. They lived down the road from Highpockets near the Hippo Branch. Bob was a train engineer and drove the train from Chattanooga to Atlanta. He would lay over in Atlanta and come back the next day. He was also mayor of Graysville in 1934. Mrs. Robinson was also the mother of Peggy who worked at the post office for many years. After her brother passed and her children were grown, Mrs. Robinson was afraid to stay alone in the house at night. My sister Peggy used to spend the nights with her. Patsy, Billy and I usually walk down to Mrs. Robinsons to meet with Peggy to catch the school bus. Sometimes when it was really cold, she let us come inside until the bus came. She was a very sweet and kind lady. Peggy was very fond of her.

LEON

Even thought he was my brother, I have to say that he grew up to be probably the meanest of all the boys. By this time, the Graham family had moved out of Graysville, otherwise Buddy would have held the title. I cannot really say they were mean. They were just full of mischief. Once Leon, along with Buddy and Butch Graham, and some of the other boys were camping at the creek down below the dam. Butch was younger than the other boys, but they let him tag along. I guess they were educating him for future pranks. They built a big roaring fire. Leon sent Butch to the sawmill to get more wood for the fire. In the summer when the creek was lower, we could walk across the top of the dam. Of course, that was one of the dangerous things we did that kept God busy watching over us. Butch carefully worked his way back across the dam with a big armload of wood, walked over, and threw it on the fire. Leon, Buddy and the other boys started jumping around, kicking the fire and swearing. Butch had no idea what he had done. Earlier that day the boys had caught a chicken and prepared it for the cookout. While Butch was gone, they started roasting it on the fire. Butch did not know about the feast they were cooking. When he returned he threw the wood on the fire, and the chicken was lost in the flames. With no chicken to eat, they broke up camp and went home.

Leon liked to catch rabbits in homemade rabbit boxes that he called a rabbit gum. I do not know if he ever trapped any or not. I do not remember seeing any, and I certainly do not remember eating any rabbits. He made the boxes out of wood with a trap door that fell shut when the rabbit entered. Once in the box, it could not get out. I don't remember if he had any bait in the box. I am sure he did not have a carrot, or I would have eaten it. Early one really cold, winter morning, after much begging to go with him, he let me tag along to check his boxes. It must have been the coldest morning of the winter. The ground was white with frost, our breath was puffing out like smoke, and I was freezing. I wanted to go back home, but he made me keep going until we checked the last box. Along the way, we passed some dried weeds with white fuzzy looking leaves and dead flowers at the top. He said the plant was rabbit tobacco. He just happened to have a paper and some matches. He picked off some leaves and made it into a cigarette, and he smoked it. I am sure it was his plan to smoke since he was prepared and knew where the plant was growing. He probably did that every morning when he went to look for rabbits, and that is why he didn't want me tagging along. Of course, there were no rabbits in the boxes, and I was glad to head back to the house. The first thing I did when we got home was tell on him for smoking rabbit tobacco. He never let me go with him again to check for rabbits. Wonder why! I still today remember what the rabbit tobacco plant looks like. I never did try smoking any. Maybe I should put that on my bucket list of things to do.

Charles Zimmerman who was Leon's brother-in-law tells about a time he went fishing with Leon down below the dam. They were out on a sand bar in the middle of the creek. The game warden appeared and wanted to check their fishing licenses. Charles did not have one, but Leon did. The game warden asks if they had licenses, and that he wanted to see them. Leon told him that he did have one, and if he wanted to see it then he could wade the creek over to where he was. The game warden started wading through the water. Leon said to Charles, "Do exactly what I say, and Charles said, ok." Then Leon said, "When he gets over here I will start running down the creek bank, and he will chase me. When we get out of sight you pick up the fishing gear and run for home." When the game warden reached the sand bar Leon took off running, and as he predicted the game warden took off after him. Charles did what he was told and grabbed the fishing gear and ran home as fast as he could. When Leon got out of sight he stopped, and the game warden asked him why he ran if he had a license. Leon pulled out his wallet and showed him the license and said, "Yes, I have a license, but the other guy with me didn't have one." This sounds like a story that would have been on the TV show, "Hee Haw." If it was, Leon probably saw the show and when the opportunity arose, he remembered and acted it out.

The sawdust pile behind the sawmill was where the local boys like to play. One of the games they played was king of the mountain. This game was to see who could be the first to climb to the top of the sawdust pile. The pile was very high. They would fight, push and pull each other down as they tried to get to the top. Whoever reached the top first was king of the mountain. They continued to do this long after they were grown. They married and had children, but when they all happened to be in Graysville at the same time the challenge was on. Once when they had been playing king of the mountain my brother stripped off his clothes to shake out the sawdust. All the other guys piled in one of their car and were leaving him behind. He ran buck-naked, jumped on the back of the car, and held on tight while they drove him through Graysville naked as a jaybird. This happened during the time a song titled, "The Streak," was popular. He waved as they passed the store. Bud said, "Look at that crazy Leon." He was living out the song and doing his streak through Graysville. I think the boys of Graysville never really grew up. The Swansons were always calling the police to come clear out the crowd that hung around the mill on the weekend. There was lots of drinking, fighting and who knows what else was going on. My brother Leon was usually right in the middle of the gang. When my younger brother Billy was around fourteen he went to the sawmill to play in the sawdust pile. He said that mom came after him and whipped him all the way home. She knew the crowd that hung around the sawmill would be a bad influence on him. I think he exaggerates about mom whipping him all the way home. Him being the baby in the family, I don't think he ever got a smack on the hand or rear end.

My brothers and sisters always talk about mom being tough and giving them whippings. The only one I ever remember getting was when I called her an old heifer because she did not let me spend the night with my friend Wilma. I rightly deserved it. I was just a kid, but old enough to know better than to call her a name like that.

MY SISTERS

Once when I was about four or five and Peggy was around seven I got a few licks in the middle of the night. Peggy and I slept together, and she cried every night. I really don't know why unless she was afraid of the dark. Maybe it was because I wet the bed and she did not want to be peed on. Anyway, mom kept telling her to stop crying, but she just kept right on. Mom told her to stop or she was going to get a spanking. Of course, she kept crying. Mom got out of bed and gave me a few licks. Afterwards, Peggy told mom that she had spanked me instead of her, so mom really gave her a spanking then. Funny thing, I slept through the whole thing and never knew. Peggy should have kept quite, but she felt guilty that I got the spanking. I guess it was just the innocence of a young child to tell the truth about what happened.

One day not long after we moved to the house on the creek, Mom decided to take us children for a walk down to the island. Earlier in the day, an airplane flew low over the house. We didn't see many planes in our area back in the fifties. It frightened Patsy so badly that she hid behind the clothes in the corner closet and would not come out. We called and called, but she never answered us. We went on with our walk, and when we came back home she finally crawled out from behind the clothes. That is when she got a few licks on her behind.

When we were young, the only time we ever got to ride in a car was when our sister Frances took us somewhere. Sometimes she took us for a ride and we stopped to get an ice cream. I always got strawberry. The most fun we had was when she took us to a drive-in moving on a Saturday night. She occasionally took us to visit Aunt Mae and Uncle Tom. They lived in Rabbit Valley, which seemed like such a long way from us. That was always a joyful time for me. I love Aunt Mae, Uncle Tom and my cousins. We always had a lot of fun. Aunt Mae had some grapevines, and when the grapes were ripe, we had a feast eating them. She always yelled out the window for us to stop eating her grapes. We just kept right on. Aunt Mae had lots of cats and dogs. I was always chasing cats to capture and play with. I liked to dress them up in whatever rags I could find. Sometimes I pinned their ears together across the top of their head with a hairpin. It is no wonder they always ran from me. They were probably thinking, "Oh no, she is back again, we better run." I think that I must have been quite a little rascal when I was young.

Mom has a Driving Lesson

My mom never learned how to drive a car. One day my brother Clay decided to give her a driving lesson. She got into the car behind the wheel; he slid in on the passenger side and proceeded to tell her what to do. We had a circle driveway that joined the road that went up to the Fryars and on down to the creek. There were some huge oak trees in the middle of that circle. She put her foot on the gas pedal, and the car took off. She rounded the circle and turned onto the road and floor-boarded the gas pedal. She headed straight for one of the big oak trees. Clay grabbed the steering wheel just as they whizzed past the tree and managed to prevent a terrible head on collision. They were both so shaken up that there was never again a mention of her learning to drive.

I took after my mom since I was twenty-five before I ever learned how to drive. For some reason no one would teach me. Peggy gave me a driving lesson, and John gave me a lesson after we were married. I must have frightened them so that they never tried to teach me to drive again. Therefore, I just taught myself. One day when John was at work and Richard was about four years old, I decided that I was going to drive the car. I put him in the back seat, got in the car and drove to Graysville. Once I got there, I was so shook-up that I turned around and went back home. It was the first time I had ever been in a car driving by myself. I never had a car of my own. Probably best that I never had one or I might have wrapped myself around a big oak tree.

THE GOAT MAN

One day Leon came running into the house yelling, "The goat man is coming, the goat man is coming!" He was so excited and wanted to go see him. We had never heard of the goat man before. He heard the news about the goat man at the store in Graysville. Mom agreed to let him ride his bike over to Highway 41 to see him. It was several miles, but it was an easy ride for him. During the forties, fifties and sixties the goat man traveled all over the country with a wagon pulled by about two dozen goats. His wagon was full of rags, a few cooking utensils and junk he picked up along the way. He traveled just a few miles a day and camped along the roadside at night. There was always a crowd of curious spectators who came out to see and talk to him. He was always friendly with them. He lived with the goats on his travels, slept with them, ate with them, and he even smelled like a goat. He was a very rugged and filthy old man. He never took a bath or washed his clothes. It was best to stay up-wind from him. The smell of him and his goats rolled into town before he did. He was always creating traffic jams along the way. He liked to tell tall tales about his adventures such as claiming to have traveled to all the states except Hawaii. The only reason he had not been there was because his goats couldn't swim. His stories were more fiction than fact. The goat man came through the Chattanooga area several times and each time creating an event, that was written up in the local newspapers. He was quite a celebrity in his day. The last time he came through Chattanooga he was mugged and ended up in the hospital. Several of his goats were killed. Leon came home telling us stories about the goat man. The stories created such imaginations in my mind, which made me want to see him even more. I could just picture him a dirty, old man curled up asleep with a bunch of goats. I never did get to see him. It usually took him several days to pass through the area, and Leon went to see him many times before he got too far away to ride his bike. He was very fascinated with the goat man. Any time the goat man came through Chattanooga on his way south you could bet that Leon was there to see him at least once. The goat man was named, Charles McCartney, and he died at the age of 97 in a nursing home in Macon, Georgia.

CLAY AND THE GREEN BANANAS

One day in the early fifties, my brother Clay came home with two huge stalks of green bananas. He heard the Graysville news that a tractor-trailer truck had wrecked on Highway 41. He took off on his bike to see what all the excitement was about. When he got there, he saw a truck filled with green bananas scattered everywhere. People were helping themselves to the bananas. Of course, he picked up two stalks and carried them home on his bike. They were almost as big as he was, and we were all amazed that he rode that far with his cargo. After a few minutes rest, he jumped back on his bike and headed out to the wreck to get more bananas. By the time he got there, they were all gone. We were excited and eager for them to turn yellow. Mom hung them up in a little house that was built next to our house. It was a playhouse for the children of the people who built the house. It was a cute little house with windows on each side of the door and on each end of the building. It was a great place for us girls to play, especially on rainy days. We liked to climb up on top of the little house and jump off. Of course, I was always barefooted and ended up with stone bruises on the bottom of my feet. We were like a bunch of monkeys climbing around on the little house while waiting for those bananas to turn yellow and ripe enough to eat. Every day we were asking mom, "Are they ripe yet." After eating all those bananas, we really did act like a bunch of monkeys fresh out of the jungle. I suppose about everyone in the Graysville area had their share of bananas

There is a bad curve on Highway 41 not far from the Tennessee and Georgia state line where many wrecks happened before the interstate was built. We called this the Otis Clark Hill or Dead Man's Curve. It was somewhere near here the banana truck wrecked. At Christmas, Mr. Clark decorated his house and grounds with hundreds or probably thousands of lights. It was so beautiful. Not many people decorated like that back in the fifties. It was always something we had to go see every year sometime during the holidays. Rumor is that Mr. Clark went to prison for income tax evasion. I suppose after paying his electric bill there was no money left to pay his taxes.

MS. BECKY EAVES

Robert Gray was a brother to, John D. Gray, and he was Ms. Becky Eaves great-grandfather. Robert's son, Charles Arthur Gray, bought and lived in the big Victorian house that Dr. Blackford built in Graysville. His daughter, Elizabeth Gray, married, Madison Rhodes, and they were parents to Ms. Becky. The Rhodes family owned a lot of land near Graysville. They lived in a big, old, farm house, and they never locked their doors. One night her parents awoke to find a man standing in their bedroom. He had just wandered into their house and was probably up to no good. They asked him what he was doing and he said, "His car was in the ditch and he needed someone to help him get it out." They told him they could not help him and to leave, and they just rolled over and went back to sleep. The next morning they found every door in the house was open and that someone had also been prowling around in the barn. The man was most likely some hobo from a train stopped on the nearby tracks.

When Ms. Becky graduated from high school, she and some of her friends decided they wanted to camp out in one of the cabins at the springs. They got permission to use the cabin, and now they had to clean it up. It was filthy. They swept, dusted and cleaned out all the debris that had been left by others. At first, it was very exciting, but once it got dark, they were so afraid that they did not sleep all night.

Ms. Eaves loves Graysville so much. I guess part of it is because her ancestors developed the community. She has such fond memories, and she is always happy to talk about the good old days in Graysville. Her greatest desire is to see someone re-store Graysville back to the days when it was a thriving little community. I think she would be contented to just sit in Graysville and watch it rain.

Years ago, one of the favorite things Mrs. Eaves used to hear people say was "A whistling girl and a crowing hen will come to no good end." I guess, back in the day that meant it was not nice for a girl to whistle. Never heard a hen crow, but many roosters I have heard.

Ms. Becky remembers the first birthday party she ever went to and it was a party for Dixie Fryar. They were in the same class in elementary school. She cannot remember if she took her a present, but hopes that she did. Dixie lived at the corner of Gunbarrel and East Brainerd Road. She went home from school with Dixie. Ms. Becky's father rode the Graysville Jitney bus to work. He had the bus stop and pick her up on his way home from work.

Ms. Becky Eaves

THE GRAYSVILLE GIRLS

The Graysville girls, as they called themselves, were friends from the time they first started elementary school. They studied and played together throughout their school years. They bonded and formed a friendship that has lasted through the years. The girls were my sister, Peggy Brock, Martha Swanson, Emily and Priscilla Rhodes, Ula Touchstone, Rebecca Self, Glenda Reavely, Melba Payne and Shirley Massengale. They usually always gathered together at Martha's house on Sundays. Sometimes they walked about three miles to Lyles Drugstore in East Brainerd to buy ice cream cones. Back in the day when they walked the road to East Brainerd they probably only had two or three cars pass them along the way. Today, it is impossible to make that trip. They would probably end up in a ditch knocked out cold. There are deep ditches right on the edge of both sides of the road. There is nowhere to get off the road when a car passes.

The girls all liked to walk to the bird sanctuary (Audubon Acres now) on Sunday afternoon. It was a long walk, but they enjoyed it and had a good time. My sister Peggy talked about one time they were rolling down the hill in an old barrel. When she took her turn, she came to a stop and could not go any farther. She crawled out of the barrel to find that she was on the edge of the creek bank with nothing but a young sapling tree holding her back.

The girls did not have cars, so there was nothing much for the them to do except go for Sunday afternoon walks. When the girls get together now the air is filled with much laughter from their reminiscing about things they used to do.

AUDUBON ACRES AND
SPRING FROG CABIN

Audubon Acres was originally the Walker Farm. Most of the land was donated to Audubon Acres by Robert Sparks Walker. The Spring Frog cabin on the property was built by the Cherokee in the 1700s. In the late sixties there was considerable damage done to the cabin by Hippies that were hanging around. The cabin was restored and a fence built around it to keep out trespassers. Spring Frog, was a Cherokee leader, of the early Indians that settled in the area of Audubon Acres along the South Chickamauga Creek. Mr. Walker donated the land to protect the family farm and to keep it preserved as a wildlife sanctuary. This is when the Audubon Acres Society was founded in 1944. Audubon Acres was first known as the Elise Chapin Wildlife Sanctuary. It is a registered site of the Trail of Tears National Historic Trail 1838. Little Owl Village is also part of Audubon Acres and is listed on the national register of historic places. Indians lived all around the area before the Indian Removable Act forced them off their land and sent them on their Death March known as the Trail of Tears.

When we were young, it was a big adventure to walk the railroad tracks to the bird sanctuary, as we called it back then. I only made the trek one time. It was a long walk for a young girl of eleven or twelve. I did visit other times after I was grown. Today Audubon Acres is a very educational place to visit. They have summer camps for children and other activities throughout the summer. It is a place of beauty with the open meadows, trees, creek, birds and other wildlife that call it their home. Many birds migrate in the spring and fall. Some like the Great Blue Heron and wood ducks live there year round. It is a great place for bird watchers to visit. It is a great place for anyone to visit. Thanks to Robert Sparks Walker for having the vision to preserve this beautiful land.

Spring Frog Cabin
Audubon Acres
Chattanooga, TN

THE BRIDGE

We were always told to never go under the bridge. Our behinds were in danger of a big bustin if our parents found out. We thought we were going straight to hell if we went under there. My friends and I wondered what in the world could be so bad under that bridge. Finally, one day when we were teenagers we decided that we could not go through life without knowing, so under we went. There was nothing there except graffiti all over the walls. It must have been the four-letter words our parents did not want us to see. Our lips were sealed, and those words, "We went under the bridge" were never spoken. Sometimes when I am at that part of the creek, I will go under the bridge. Maybe next time, I will take a can of spray paint and write, "Shirley was here."

That old bridge holds a special place in my heart. That is where John proposed to me. He picked me up after work one day. When we crossed the bridge at Graysville, he turned off the road into an open field where people parked their cars while they went fishing or swimming. We got out of the car and walked around. Then he pulled the ring out of his pocket and popped the question. When he tried to put it on my finger, it was too small. I was so embarrassed that it did not fit. I was also embarrassed because I thought that I had such big fingers. I cried and cried. I didn't know how to express my feelings and he didn't know what was wrong. I guess he was beginning to regret the whole thing and wish that he had never asked me to marry him. Today, I tell him that if he had only known what he was getting into he would still be running. Thinking back, maybe I was crying because I wanted a bigger diamond. Several of my friends who had gotten married about that time all had big one carat diamond rings and here I was with maybe a half-carat. I should have known right then that I was going to marry a man that would not easily part with his money. Anyway, that little ole diamond has served me well.

I do not know how many bridges were built across the Chickamauga Creek in that area. Mr. Gray built a wooden bridge that was burned during the Civil War. Mr. Gray must have re-built the bridge that lasted until a bridge was built around 1920. After the new, wide bridge was built in 1981, the old bridge is now used as a walking bridge. The new bridge is wide enough for two cars to pass and then walking room along the sides. The old bridge was a one-lane bridge, and cars had to wait if another car was crossing. The road from the bridge to the railroad crossing dipped down, and when the creek got up it was always under water. When the new bridge was built, the roadbed was filled in and raised to prevent the water from getting over the road. However, once one crossed over the railroad tracks the road goes down hill, and it is much lower on that side of the tracks. This is where the water backs up over the road. Somewhere near the Hippo Branch, there is an opening for the water to flow under the road and railroad into the creek. That is where the creek water backs out onto the road and keeps traffic from going into Graysville. The water covering the road is too deep for cars to drive through. Occasionally, when we have lots of rain the water backs up all the way to the Graysville store. Swanson Road, formerly the Holler Road, also crosses Hurricane Creek a few miles from Graysville. The water gets over the road there, and no one can get into Graysville from that direction. Therefore, you can't get there when the creek rises

THE OLD BRIDGE

Nicknames

Almost everyone that ever lived in Graysville had a nickname. Pete and Bud were responsible for many of these names. Sam Salty is the nickname I find the most amusing and would love to know the origin, but probably never will. How in the world did he ever come by that name? As far as I know, his name was not Sam, and I always wondered if he liked salt. We had a lot of bears living in Graysville. There was Barefoot, Bearcat, Bearface and probably other bears I do not recall. A few of the nicknames are Cotton, YoYo, Unk, Bugger Joe, Red, Roundy, Big Boy, Long Distance, and his twin brothers we called the Jerrys, Fifty, Butch, Buddy, Hopper, Dude, Bunk, Poodle, Pig, Petey, Highpockets, Junebug, Ronnie Red, Bingham, Blackie, Myrtle, also know as Robert Tree, Poodle, Bunny, Tangy, Hawk, Poss and many more. Last, but not least Pete and Bud are on this list of nicknames since their names were William and James. Most of these have passed on and left their legends behind. They were all one of a kind and will not be forgotten.

THE DOG DAYS OF SUMMER

The dog days of summer begin in the middle of July and last until the middle of August. Dog days are the hottest and most humid days of the summer. Even though it is the hottest and driest time of the year, there is always a thunderstorm somewhere in the area. Dog days are named after the dog star Sirius. It is the brightest star in the sky. It rises and sets with the sun during dog days. There are many myths about dog days. Some of them are: snakes go blind, fish won't bite, wounds won't heal and dogs go mad. I don't know about those blind snakes. If I see one, I will not stick around to find out if it is blind. I will run away as fast as possible. For me dogs days meant that I could not go swimming. I don't know why we were not supposed to swim during that time. However, there were many times we did swim during dog days, and it didn't kill us. We were told that we would get sick if we went in the water. I always thought that perhaps because the days were so hot it caused the water to get warmer. The warmer water caused more bacteria to grow, which could make us sick. What did I know! As a kid, I hated dog days more than Pig Plemons and the Fryar boys. I had nothing else to do during these hot and sultry, lazy days of summer except go swimming. Besides begging to go to the creek, another annoying thing I did was go around talking Pig Latin all the time. This must have been a time in the summer that mom's nerves were tested to the limits. I am sure she was wishing it was time for school to start.

A Few Graysville
People I Remember

Leslie Anderson - Back in the forties, fifties and early sixties, one could always tell it was the beginning of a new school year by the new dark blue, denim jeans and overalls the boys were wearing. They had new crisp, plaid, cotton, button-up shirts. Leslie Anderson and his brother Vernon were always shined up like a new penny in their new clothes. I remember seeing them get on and off the school bus at Dug Road and think what a long walk they had to catch the bus. I remember when my brothers were teenagers they did not want to wear overalls. They wanted jeans. By the end of the school year, their clothes were faded with holes, which were patched on the knees and the seat of their pants. When the boys outgrew their clothes they were handed down to the younger brothers. This was also true with the younger girls in a family. The younger siblings' lot in life was to wear hand-me-downs. Back then it was always embarrassing to wear patched clothing, but today they would be right in style with big holes in their jeans.

Kenneth Childers - The Graysville sawmill was a place of employment for many local men. It was also a place of entertainment for the local boys on the weekend. Kenneth worked at the sawmill when he was in high school. After graduating, he continued working there for about a year until he was drafted into the army. After returning home from the army, he went back to work at the sawmill. He soon decided that there were better things to do in life, so he took advantage of the college program offered by the government and went back to school. Good for him.

Fred McCary - I don't know if I am spelling his name correct or not. He has been gone for a long time, so I guess it will be ok since he will not be around to correct me. He worked at the barrel factory. He was a very ornery old man. The young boys used to throw his lawn furniture up in the trees just to make him mad, and it certainly did. Maybe he had a reason to be grumpy. I always hated to go to the store when he was there, especially if he was coming out the door as I was going in. He grumbled about something all the time. He was related to Fifty McCary, and he was just as grumpy as Fred. They would start big arguments in the Graysville store and sometimes were told to leave.

The Bennetts - Berry and Mamie Lou Bennett moved to Graysville from two small communities named Ramhurst and Ballground near the Chatsworth, and Dalton, Georgia area. Mr. Bennett's grandfather was part Cherokee Indian. When they married, they moved to Dalton to be close to Mr. Bennett's job at Crown Carpet Mill. Later he got a job at the T&T Plant, and they moved to Hixson, Tennessee. Sometime later they moved to Graysville and lived in several different houses until Mr. Bennett took a job in Atlanta. Mrs. Bennett hated Graysville; but after living in Atlanta for a while, she was happy to get back to Graysville. They bought the big Graysville house and lived there many years. Mrs. Bennett started and was in charge of the cafeteria at the old school house. They had two children, Geraldine and Billy. Geraldine remembers on school days when they had peanut butter crackers because she and her brother had to help their mother make them. Billy was in the Navy and the heartthrob of many Graysville girls. Geraldine married Sonny Whitlow, and they have two children, Cheryl and Cotton. Cotton lived in Graysville until a few years ago when he and his wife Robin bought a new house and moved. Geraldine says that Cotton loves Graysville so much that he would live in a tent if he could go back. Geraldine had a beautiful yellow prom dress, and several of the girls in Graysville borrowed her dress to wear to their prom. Prom dresses were expensive back then, just as they are today. Most all the girls borrowed one if they could. Geraldine and her friend Wilma did not have a date for the prom, so Geraldine borrowed her dad's car and drove them. After they left home, two boys came and wanted to take them. She never did find out who the boys were. Geraldine always had a lot of girlfriends that spent the night with her, and they had so much fun at these sleepovers. Dave Brown was the first person in Graysville to get a television, and the Bennetts were the second. They always had a house full of people watching television with them. My brother Leon talked about getting to watch television with them sometimes. Other times, he and some of his friends sat out on the edge of their yard and watched the television through the window. They didn't consider themselves as being "peeping toms." They just wanted to watch television.

Sandy and Nezzie Harwood - Sandy was a barber in Chattanooga, and he rode the bus to work. Mrs. Harwood drove him out to the corner of Graysville Road and East Brainerd Road to catch the bus. She went back and pick him up in the afternoon. They were very nice people and the parents of my long time childhood friend Martha. Martha had two younger brothers Charlie and Jeff and a younger sister Sara. She had two older brothers Jim and Allen. On Sundays we all walked home from church together. We could have taken a short cut across the railroad, but we always chose to walk on down to were our road crossed the railroad tracks. We wanted to spend more time with them because Jeff and Charlie were so funny. Jeff was a real little ham, and Charlie was a cute little fellow who was always trying to keep up with his brother. It was a very sad time in our lives when Jeff got sick with cancer. We were all just young children. It was the first time we had experienced death, and since he was our age it was more traumatic. Jeff was sadly missed for many years, especially when we walked home from church without him.

Ms. Bates - She was my second grade teacher in the old three-room school house. She had a son, John Brown, that was meaner than anyone we had every met. They lived just across the road from where our dirt road crossed over the railroad tracks. Sometimes they came over to visit us. He broke off big switches and hit us with them. He also pinched us and pulled our hair. We could not do anything about it when his mother was with him; but when he came alone, we really paid him back. We all got big switches and beat up on him. He always went home crying. They finally moved away, and we were glad to see them go.

Harold Anderson - My first memory of Harold was when I started first grade. This was before we moved to the little house on the creek beside the school. It was the first day of school, and mom was walking with us to go register. When we passed Harold's house, his mother and father were backing out of the driveway to take him to school. They asked if we wanted a ride, and mom was glad for the offer since she was carrying my brother who was just a baby. Part of the time she also carried my younger sister who was only three years old, and I was just five. It was about a mile walk to the school, which was too far for young children to walk. We happily crawled into the back seat, and to me it seemed to be such a big car. That was my first memory of riding in a car, and it was my last memory of Harold until I was in third grade. By the time I was in third grade we were living in the little house beside the school. When I started third grade the class was split up into two rooms. Harold, Billy Joe and I were the only ones in the same room with the first and second graders. The other third graders were in the room with the fourth and fifth graders. Since we lived close to the school I always went home for lunch. One day, I asked Harold if he wanted to go home with me for lunch, and he accepted the invite. We went to the house and there was nothing to eat. Mom was out washing clothes and had not fixed anything for my lunch. I don't know what she gave us to eat. I guess it was a leftover biscuit from breakfast. She was so mad at me and told me to never bring anyone home for lunch again. She said that she was too busy to cook and also we did not have enough food to feed an extra person. One day the teacher told us to study our spelling. I was reading a story in a book and did not want to stop. Harold told me to put my book inside the speller and prop it up on my desk. It looked like I was studying my spelling. I got so engrossed in the story that I let my spelling book slip down, and the teacher could see that I was reading. Of course, I got a scolding for not studying my spelling. Harold was my first boyfriend. One day he gave me some peanut butter crackers and a little tin cup if I would be his girlfriend. Of course, I could not refuse those peanut butter crackers. Later that afternoon, my mom wanted to know where I got the cup, and I told her. She fussed at me and said that I was too little for boyfriends and to give it back. The next day Harold got the cup back, but he didn't get the crackers.

Omalee Griffin - She and I were best friends when we started first grade. Neither one of us had ever been away from home, and we both hated school. We both cried every day. The teacher had her brother Bo and my sister Peggy to come sit with us in hopes of getting us to stop crying. Once, Omalee got behind the classroom door and cried. Bo came in and got behind the door with her. Some days she cried so much that the teacher let him take her home. I looked out the window and saw them walking down the road. I wondered why the teacher would not let me go home. This went on for several days at the beginning of the school year. Omalee sat beside me, and one day I saw a puddle beside her desk. She had wet her pants. It wasn't long before there was a puddle beside my desk. We were too afraid to ask the teacher to let us go to the bathroom. I don't know if we were afraid to ask the teacher or if we were more afraid to go to the outdoor outhouse.

Gertrude Rhodes - She was a loyal and faithful member of the Graysville Methodist Church. Everyone, especially the children, loved her. We all called her Granny Rhodes. She was so sweet to everyone and was always wearing a smile. She was a relative of Ms. Eaves whose parents owned the Rhodes Farm not far from the church. Ms. Eaves remembers the children calling her Aunt Dirty. They did not understand that the grownups were saying Aunt Gertie. She along with the other grownups thought it was so funny to hear the children say Aunt Dirty. Granny Rhodes' granddaughter Priscilla told me that Granny used to say, "Pretty fades, but ugly last forever."

Lillian Ward - She lived in a big two-story, pre-civil war house on Gray Street. When she reached those golden years, she was afraid to stay by herself. Rebecca stayed with her at night, and Martha took over when Rebecca could no longer stay. Some people say the house is haunted. I would be afraid to stay there even with a dozen people in the house. My nephew Robert now owns the house and lived there for several years. His sister Robbie presently lives in the house. In the old days when the Wards lived there, borders occasionally stayed with them. That was a way to make a little extra money when times were hard.

Orville and Virginia Heard moved to Graysville around 1958. They were very nice people. They lived in the Vaughan house at the end of Graysville where Swanson Road begins. A few years later they moved downtown Graysville in a huge house across the street from my brother. Mr. Heard sometimes took my mom to the store when she didn't want to wait for one of her children to take her. Viola was one of the pretty girls that lived in Graysville. She always had such beautiful hair. It was blonde and thick with just the right amount of curls. Her friend, Judy Mulleur, likes to claim she lived in Graysville because she spent so much time at Viola's house. Viola and Judy became best friends when Judy moved over and let her sit beside her on the school bus. Viola and my sister Pat were always good friends. Pat remembers Viola's mother teaching her how to make the best sandwich in the world. It was fried spam with a slice of cheese, mayo, lettuce and a big slice of tomato on toasted bread. Viola and her friends were always playing tin-can shinny, hide-and-seek and other games in the street by her house. One time Viola had a slumber party with Judy, Pat and some other girls. They were all in shorty pajamas making candy when a car load of boys stopped at her house. Her mother kept the boys outside while the girls ran and changed clothes. That was a time of giggles by a bunch of teenage girls.

Gene Cavin - was the man who moved us from Hawkinsville back to Graysville. In that old truck, we must have looked like the Clampetts when they moved to Hollywood. My mom had written her brother Tom about what a hard time she was having living with my abusive, alcoholic dad. He hired Gene to move us to live with him and his family. It cost $75.00 dollars to move us. Gas must have really been cheap back in those days. I am so thankful she was brave enough to leave that horrible man and start a new life. Mom never re-married nor did she ever have a boyfriend. She was such a good person. Her life was taking care of us children. Funny how things happen in life. When my brother Robert married and had a family, his son married Gene's daughter. Robert, Jr. says that if Gene had know that his daughter would grow up to marry Robert's son he would have left us in Hawkinsville.

My Brothers - One thing my brothers liked to do was play the game of marbles. They always had a pocket full of marbles. Their prize possession was a large marble about three times the size of a regular marble and it was called a shooter. The marbles were so pretty with many different colors. I don't recall exactly how the game was played. What I remember is they drew a circle in the dirt and put their marbles inside the circle. They took turns trying to shoot the marbles out of the circle. I guess they got to keep the ones they shot out. Sometimes they were disappointed when they lost some of their favorite marbles to other players. They had to be a good sport to play this game because they were taking a risk of losing their favorite marbles, especially their shooter.

These are a few of the people I remember from the past that lived in Graysville: Mrs. Sansing who was part Indian. She lived in a little barn apartment on the corner of the Bennett's property. She took in washing and ironing from people along with babysitting to support herself. Others were Ditty and Henry Roberson and their son Henry who we sometimes called Little Henry or Hank just to make him mad, Bob Self, Roosie and Hazel Touchsone, Cecil Dalton Bynum, the daughter of Dr. Dalton, John and Elvera Simpson, Mrs. Cavin who was a tiny little woman and wore a sunbonnet like in the old days. She was the mother of Frankie who was married to Bud Brown. There was Dave Brown, brother of Pete and Bud and their sister Mary and their mother. They also had a sister Emily who was married to Earl Bowling. The Hensley's, Luke, Harm, Annie and Bob Alice. They lived beside the store in a very old spooky house, like the one in the movie, "To Kill A Mocking Bird."

These are a few people I know who presently live in Graysville: My brother Bill and Pam, Ronnie and Tonya, Crissy Crawford, Peggy Swanson, Delores and Bill Clifford, Kenneth Childers, Jan Poole, Carolyn and Jack Towns, Mrs. Poston, Viola, Robin Armstrong, Dale Fryar. Of course, I have probably left out a few and for that please accept my apology.

Across the tracks from the little house on the creek were three houses owned by the railroad. In one of the houses is where my friend Wilma Self lived. It was a big frame house with a porch across the front facing the railroad. She and I sat on the front porch cutting paper dolls out of the Sears catalog while watching the trains pass by. Sometimes a gang of us played ball in her yard. One time the ball came down on top of her dad's head and that ended the game. After that was when we started playing ball in the Fryar's back yard.

One of my fondest memories of Graysville are the dirt roads. Front Street, the main drag through Graysville, was paved as far back as I can remember. The side streets were dirt and sent up a cloud of dust every time a car passed. Finally, in 1962 the side roads were paved. It was wonderful when windows could be washed and stay clean for a reasonable time. I remember my friend Pansy came to visit one time and she said, "I like your house, but you need to wash the windows." I told her it did not do much good with the dust blowing in the wind after the cars passed. Anyway, what did she know about keeping windows clean. She was from Soddy-Daisy! Some people tend to speak before they think. Why do I have fond memories of the dirt roads? I just like dirt roads. Maybe it takes me back to the little dirt road to our house on the creek and all those days I spent playing in the dirt when I was a child.

There were many large families in Graysville through the years. It must have been because of the trains passing through in the middle of the night blowing their loud horns. It woke up the old men and they had their way in the dark and probably didn't even remember it the next day. That might possibly be the cause of so many large families.

TRAIN DERAILS
AT THE TRESTLE

It was sometime around 1966 or '67 when a train derailed crossing the trestle in Graysville. Several box cars fell into the creek. All kinds of merchandise was floating around in the water. There were televisions, jewelry, towels, other linens, silverware, and all kinds of things being shipped from Spiegel and Sears catalogs. People of Graysville, along with outsiders who heard about the derailment, were all down there pulling things out of the creek. My brother Bill pulled out a big bundle of towels and washcloths. He traded them to Petey Swanson for two pairs of pants for himself.

Mrs. Poston said that they were eating breakfast when they heard the train derail. It was such a loud noise, and they had no idea what had happened. Mac went out to see what was going on, and he saw people walking down the railroad tracks. He saw that the train had jumped the tracks and several box cars had fallen into the creek. Mac was too excited to go to work, so he stayed home and spent much of the day at the site of the wreck. Mrs. Poston said that Mac brought her some pillowcases with a design on them that needed to be embroidered. A short time later he came back to the house with embroidery thread. She did the embroidery work on the pillowcases and still has them. That was the only train wreck in Graysville all the years we lived there. I was always afraid one would fall off the tracks and roll across the road and into our house. That was one of my greatest fears. Never happened!

In the past the railroad lowered the water for inspections of the trestle. I suppose that today they have underwater equipment to do the job. When they inspected the trestle, the water was lowered by opening a gate at the gristmill next to the dam. Kenneth Childers tells about looking off the bridge in Graysville when the water was down. He saw metal supports from the old bridge sticking up out of the water. He said, "He would never jump off the bridge after seeing them." People still jump off the bridge today just as I did back in my young days. I was old enough to know better than to jump, but still young enough to enjoy the thrill. It was a stupid thing for me to do.

Two Big Fish

Up and down the banks of the Chickamauga Creek in Graysville is a great place to fish. Once my brother Robert caught a thirty plus pound catfish somewhere near the trestle. Everyone in Graysville was excited because they had never seen a fish that big caught there in the creek. Pictures were taken, and one found a place on the wall in the Brown Brothers' Store. That record lasted for many years until Cotton caught a sixty plus pound catfish somewhere near the old gristmill and dam. Those fish were big enough to have a fish fry that would have fed the whole community.

Robert Brock

NO PHOTO
The other big fish got away.

MEMORIES LIVE ON

Once I started writing about Graysville, I have come to realize that the Graysville people from long ago will continue to live on through telling the stories of their lives. Also, many of the people who still live there today will have their stories passed down to future generations, and my brother Bill will be included. He is probably the most colorful character in Graysville at the present time. Mr. Gray being the most notable person will always be remembered since Graysville was named after him. The most notorious person was Fred Vaughan. My brother Bill, the keeper of the springs, is one that will be talked about years after he is gone. He is so smart and comes up with the funniest sayings and ideas. He is well known for his signs. He puts up signs going down the little dirt road to the springs. They say such things as, "Trespassers will be shot, and survivors will be shot again." Some of the little boys in the neighborhood really believe what his signs say. They take off on their bikes in the opposite direction when they see him. One of his favorite things to do is take a long twisted gourd and tie it onto a long cane. It looks like a fishing pole with a giant worm. He goes over to the bridge and pretends to be fishing. People passing by in cars see his huge pole and stop to ask if he is catching anything. They get their cameras out, take pictures of his big pole and worm, and marvel at his artistry. Everyone who knows him loves him. They will agree that he is certainly one of a kind.

After seeing all the work my brother did at the springs, I think he should restore Gray's Island. I might even help him chop down a tree or two. If he cut away all the trees and scrubby plants the creek could wash back some of the gravels it washed away. Who knows what he might find. Perhaps, he would find some of the bones from the old cow and sheep that washed up on the island years ago. He would probably find a few arrowheads. He might find the old sulfur spring we passed on the way down to the island. The water was orange, dark, oily looking and smelled like rotten eggs. I don't know how anyone could ever drink sulfur water. However, it is suppose to have some good health benefits by providing minerals the body needs. He just might find the rest of the bones left behind after Mrs. Fryar found a petrified fox head on Gray's Island. Gray's Island may hold a few surprises like Edgewater Beach. There might be a clear water spring or two waiting to be uncovered. We always thought that there was just one spring; but when Bill cleaned out the wild growth, he found two more springs. He cleaned them up, and the water is crystal clear. He also found a lemon tree growing on the opposite side of the springs. Each summer we look for the yellow lemons. They are so sour we cannot eat them. My brother drinks from the springs almost every day and says it is better than the water from the faucet in his kitchen sink. People camping at the springs also drink and use the spring water.

I recently took Ms. Eaves down to the springs, and she was in awe of how it has changed. She looked all around and talked about how she remembered the cabins on the hill, the springs and the creek. She remembered the boat dock and other things built by Fred Vaughan. She is presently 93 years old and has a mind like an elephant. The old saying is, "Elephants remember everything." She remembered how cold the spring water was back then. I gave her some spring water in a cup, and she put her hand in it and said, "Yes, it is still cold." Just as happy as I was to see Gray's Island, she was just as excited to see her childhood playground.

Edgewater Beach
Graysville, Georgia

REMEMBER THE PAST

As I write these words, they flood my mind with memories of yesterday. Sometimes it is good to let our minds travel back in time and remember the good old days. Of course, it is not good to live in the past. However, it is always good to remember the days of our parents, Indians, no electricity and what life was like in that period of time. It makes us more appreciative of what we have today. In our fast-paced world with all the high tech phones, computers, ipads and other electronic equipment, it is easy to speed through life and forget about the past. It is like the old adage, "Take time to smell the roses." We need to take time to look back and let our minds wander through the history of our parents, grandparents and other ancestors. It is so interesting to think about how they lived and thrived a hundred years ago. It is hard to believe how our ancestors carved out an existence in the wilderness of Graysville and how they ever survived. It was pure perseverance that kept them going. Hard work was all they knew back then, and they made the best of a difficult situation. I remember my mom washing clothes in an old black iron pot. She built a fire under it to heat the water. In the winter, the clothes would sometimes freeze as we hung them on the clothesline. Letting my mind drift back into the old days, especially of Graysville, leaves me with bittersweet yet warm feelings of my early childhood. I hope this book will inspire you to recall stories of your youth and the similar predicaments you experienced during your young years.

If these stories sound familiar to some of you, and most of them probably do, I hope that I have something new to say that make them still enjoyable to read. I have done my best to preserve the accuracy of Graysville history and stories. I hope you have enjoyed reading these pages as I traveled on my journey through by-gone days of Graysville and my life as a young child growing up in a community of extraordinary people.

GRANDCHILDREN STORIES

I must include a few funny stories about my grandchildren. Actually, they are the reason I am writing this book and the previous book, Gray's Island, Where the Creek Bends. I wanted to record some of my life stories to pass down to them so they will know what it was like back in Grandma's day. They think of me as a dinosaur, and after reading these stories it will confirm their thoughts.

William and Mary Grace, the twins - They just turned seven in November 2014. They were sitting in the living room floor giggling and giggling. Their mother Alice decided that she might need to check on all those giggles. When she came close to the door, she heard them telling stories about things they did when they were little. They are only seven and talking about what they used to do. One of them said, "Do you remember the time we called Onstar when mommy was pumping gas? The lady told us not to call Onstar unless our mommy was in the car." They burst into giggles again. Alice stepped into the room and said, "No, I don't remember that, and the look on their face was priceless."

John Patrick - Once when John Patrick was about five years old, he was coming home with me to visit for a few days. He asked me what the rule on Sprite was at my house. I thought for a minute and said, "John Patrick, I don't have any rules on Sprite at my house." Then I asked him, "What are the rules at your house?" He replied that he could have five or six Sprites a day. I told him that he could have as many Sprites as he wanted at Grandma's house. Of course, I would never let him have more than one a day. His parents are very strict about him eating healthy, and Sprite was allowed about once a week. At this early age, he was already learning how to get what he wanted.

Jason Alan - When Jason was eight years old, he was visiting for a few days. John walked through the house, and some dishes in a cabinet rattled.

He walked back through, and they rattled again. Jason was sitting at the table eating a bowl of cereal. He looked at me and said, "How much does Granddaddy weigh? Every time he walks through the house the dishes rattle." I told him that I did not know and he should ask him. John came through the kitchen again. As Jason continued to eat he never looked up and said, "I wonder what that guy weighs!" It was so funny to hear him refer to his granddad as that guy.

Elizabeth (Beth) - When Pete and Alice lived in Georgia, I loved to go down and baby-sit. They had my first grandchild, and that was a wonderful time in my life. One day I was cleaning in the kitchen, and Beth was in the living room playing. Occasionally, I would step around the corner to check on her. I noticed that it had become very quite so I decided to check on her again. Somewhere she had found a box of crayons and was drawing all over the big screen television. I quickly got a towel and started cleaning the screen, but the stuff did not want to come off. I worked very hard until it was not noticeable when the TV was on. However, when it was off, one could see faint marks on the black screen. I said, "Beth, if you don't tell, neither will I." Of course, she was too young to know what I was saying, but she did not get into trouble. I blamed myself for not watching her more closely.

My grandchildren are such a joy to me. I could write a book about them, but not this time.

My precious grandchildren left to right Beth, Mary Grace,
John Pactick, William, Jason and Grandma standing

The Springs at Edgewater Beach

John and Shirley at Edgewater Beach

My dog Dixie Reed Turney 8 years old

My favorite nephew Donnie

Chickamauga Creek photo made from the bridge

Spring Frog Cabin Audubon Acres Chattanooga, TN

Holly and Josh at Edgewater Beach

All that's left of Gray's Island

The Trestle at Edgewater Beach

Ms. Becky and Shirley at Edgewater Beach

Old Mining & Manufacturing Building
Small building was a school house in 1900

Old Lime Kiln

Graysville Cemetery

IN THE FOREFRONT GENERAL RICHARD W. JOHNSON AT GRAYSVILLE

The General Monument

Old Graysville Three-Room School House

Eugene Bynum and
Cecil Dalton Bynum

Old Graysville Depot

Pete and Bud Brown's Store

Beautiful house made from the old grist mill

Old Mill

Mining and manufacturing workers 1903

Josh and Holly paddling around in the muddy Chickamauga Creek.

The Keeper of the Springs

POEMS

QUILTING IN THE DARK

By: Shirley Turney
June 30, 2014

She sat there in her chair gently rocking back and forth.
Her hair was pulled up into a knot on top of her head.
Her glasses slid down on her nose as she sat there
Quilting in the dark.

Her hands and fingers ached with each stitch she made.
However, there were more quilts to make for cold nights ahead.
She said, "Everyone needs a quilt for their bed," so she just kept on
Quilting in the dark.

The lamp light over her shoulder shinned bright, but
To her the room was dim and she could hardly see.
Her eyes were tired and weak from years of
Quilting in the dark.

People asked why she kept making so many quilts.
Because making quilts is my gift from God,
And I cannot stop, so she just kept on
Quilting in the dark.

The grandchildren love to look through her stack of quilts
And pick out their favorite ones under which to sleep.
There are many quilts she still wants to make so she keeps
Quilting in the dark.

Many people have been blessed with one of her quilts.
How many more can she make is the question?
The answer is as long as her clock keeps ticking she will keep
Quilting in the dark.

A LITTLE BOY

By: Shirley Turney
March 24, 2014

He is just a little boy
So full of life and
Ever so happy.

You will always see a smile
On his face, but a piece of
Candy he will not taste.

He loves his chicken nuggets and
Fries with ketchup on the side.
Never is a crumb left on his plate.

All those nuggets and fries are
What makes him so smart and
Such a handsome young boy.

He is always good and never
Gets into trouble...well maybe
Just a little sometimes.

But he cannot help it.
He may sometimes misspeak,
Or forget to do his chores.

Therefore, parents remember to be kind.
You were little once upon a time.
He is just a little boy.

Written for John Patrick after getting into trouble one day.

JASON'S POEM

By: Shirley Turney
May 7, 2014

Jason, my son, where are you today?
Are you flying around from cloud to cloud
Smiling down on me?
When a raindrop splashes on my face,
Is that you crying for me, or is it
Because you are happy and free?
When the sun shines warm on my skin,
Is that you sending down your love to
Fill my heart with memories of
All the good times we had.
I do not understand why you had to go so soon,
But you really did not leave me because
Your spirit is always by my side.
I can hear you say, "Dad don't grieve
For me, enjoy each beautiful day
God has given you, and
One day we will be together again."
I know you are in God's hands, and
He has made a beautiful place for you,
Even prettier than the springs.
For now, I will sit by my springs and smile
While I think about you.
You are always in my heart giving
Me the strength to make it through another day.
Until we meet again, I will always remember,
My son, that I am so proud of and
Who I will always love and never forget.

Billy Jason Brock
May 26, 1978 - July 9, 2013

Written for my brother and his beloved son
Jason. I tried to put into words
how I think my brother feels about the loss of his son.

Winter is not Over Yet

By: Shirley Turney
March 9, 2014

On the other side of the fence where the grass grows greener,
And the daffodils bloom a deeper yellow, it makes me think that
Spring is just around the corner.

Tiny little purple and yellow crocus barely stick their heads out of the
Ground to soak up the long awaited warmth of the sun.

Reality tells me that it is just early March, and there is more cold weather
Yet to come. I can verify this prediction by the tulip tree that is about to
Bloom. Just over the horizon, there is more bad weather on the loom.

There is cold and ice, or even snow just waiting to nip
Those beautiful pink flowers in the bud.

Mother Nature plays this mean trick on us every year.
She loves to make us think that spring has finally sprung,
Only to slap us in the face with a wind so cold we shiver and shake.

Put away the rake and garden tools. Go back
inside and sit by the fire while
You sip on something warm. Winter is not over yet.

Almost every year the beautiful tulip tree
across the street blooms and then
we get a big frost that turns the beautiful pink blooms brown.

ARE YOU READY

By: Shirley Turney
December 22, 2013

On the horizon, the sun is waking up.
Time to start a new day.
Are you ready?

As always, a busy day awaits.
If the challenges are hard to face,
Are you ready?

There are many choices to be made,
What or when to eat, work or play.
Are you ready?

Christmas is just around the corner.
Have you wrapped the presents, baked the cookies and cakes,
Are you ready?

When the sun goes down and the day's work is done,
And it is time for bed and a good night's sleep,
Are you ready?

When the trumpet's sound can be heard around the world,
And the clouds roll back and Jesus appears,
Are you ready?

Written Sunday, December 22, 2013 after Pastor Tom ended his
sermon by saying, "Are you ready?"

A TURNEY MAN

By: Shirley Turney
June 8, 2014

God bless the woman who marries a Turney man.
Double bless her if he is an electrical engineer.

John said that I better not write this poem so I stopped.
I thought maybe I had said enough in these two lines, and
there was no need to write anymore. Funny, I should
write this on our anniversary the 8th of June.

THE DARK SIDE
OF THE MOON

By: Shirley Turney
March 24, 2014

Do not worry about me after I grow old.
There will be words I cannot recall
And faces I do not remember.
Just pick me up when I stumble and fall.

It's ok if I walk out the door
Never to be seen any more.
I do not know why,
But I have to roam.

So when I get lost in this world
And cannot find my way, I will be fine.
For me, there will be no tomorrows or yesterdays
But you will remember for me.

When that day comes my mind will be far away.
If you miss me and wonder where I am,
On this planet I will not be.
Just look for me on the dark side of the moon.

This poem is dedicated to friends who have been afflicted
with that terrible disease known as Alzheimer's.

CHICK-A-MELON

By: Shirley Turney
June 30, 2014

Here deep in the South
Where the watermelons grow,
And the chickens cross the road,
We love to eat our favorite foods.
Fried chicken and watermelon.
That is why we love our chick-a-melon.

Written for my brother, Bill Brock, to go with his drawings
and paintings of Chick-A-Melons

Chic-A-Melon
Drawing by: Bill R. Brock

BURY ME IN BLACK

By: Shirley Turney
October 18, 2014

Bury me in black
Beneath an old weeping willow tree.
No yellow, green, red or blue
Dress do I need.

Just a plain old black one
Will do just fine.
Black to blend in with that
Deep dark place where I will sleep.

At first, all will come to visit my grave
And bring me flowers of every kind,
But as times goes by the busy world
Will keep you away.

So do not feel bad if you do not come.
Your life must go on after I am gone.
Just think of me sometimes.
I will have that old willow tree to weep for me.

Don't know why I thought of this poem unless it
is because my birthday is just a few days away and
I feel time is slipping by too quickly.

WAR EAGLE

By: Shirley Turney
August 2013

First of September when the leaves begin to turn,
On the plains of Alabama, it is football time.
So once again, we hear the War Eagle cry.
The stadium is filled with students
And people from all walks of life.
They are here to watch the tigers play and
To see the War Eagle fly.

I wrote this for my family. We always eagerly await
the start of football season. WAR EAGLE!!!!!!!!!!!!

This is my favorite poem. Even though it was in
my other book, I just had to include it again.

Without Ms. Eaves sharing her memories with me, this book would not exist. She is a wonderful person, and it is an honor and a privilege to know her. I can think of no better way to end this book than to give her the credit she so rightfully deserves. Thank you, Ms. Becky Eaves.

Ms. Becky and Shirley

I hope this book leaves you hungry for more stories about Graysville.

ECCLESIASTES 1:4

4 One generation passeth away, and another generation cometh:
but the earth abideth forever.

Just as the Bible says, "generations come and go" so do the
generations of Graysville, and like the earth Graysville still abides.

25444560R00090

Made in the USA
Middletown, DE
30 October 2015